5

Le Guide di Terra Ferma

With the patronage of the Region of Veneto

Regione del Veneto

Provincia di Vicenza

Comune di Bassano del Grappa

Le Guide di Terra Ferma
Series directed by Giuseppe Barbieri

Many thanks for the helpfulness to
Lino Manfrotto

Translations
Denise Jeffrey
Michi Fontana

Tel 049.9930254, fax 049.9933273
E-mail info@terra-ferma.it

Printing by: Grafiche Antiga - Cornuda (TV)

ISBN 88-87760-20-9

Bassano del Grappa

texts by

Giuseppe Barbieri

PHOTOGRAPHS

Archivio Andolfatto, *pic. 119*

Archivio Fotografico della Soprintendenza per i Beni Artistici e Storici del Veneto, Verona *pic. 12-13, and pages 62-63.*

Archivio Poli Museo della Grappa: *pic. 133-136, 138.*

Archivio Terra Ferma
pic. 18, 20, 27-28, 34, 36, 67-68, 72-76, 83, 85, 106, 113-115, 128, 141, 149-152, and page 62.

Bassano del Grappa (a cura di Gina Fasoli), Bologna 1988, *pic. 4*

Mario Bozzetto, *pic. 19, 60, 69-70, 82, 98, 101-102, 104.*

Cesare Gerolimetto
pp. 8-9; *pic. 5, 8, 10, 22-23, 26, 29, 38, 49-50, 59, 79, 81, 84, 108, 117, 121-123, 125-127, 140, 142, 147, 159-164.*

Museo Biblioteca Archivio di Bassano del Grappa
pic. 1-3, 6, 11, 15-16, 21, 31, 33, 35, 39-42, 47-48, 63-64, 80, 86, 88-89, 91-93, 110, 118, 120, 129-132, 139;
pic. 9 (Andrea Fasoli)
pic. 14, 24, 30, 32, 44-45, 61-62, 65, 71, 90, 95-97, 105, 107, 109, 111-112, 116, 124, 137, 143-146, 148 (Andrea Bergozza);
pic. 37 (Oscar Ganzina)
pic. 46 (Foto Alessio)
pic. 51-56 (Foto Tomba)
pic. 57 (Riccardo Urnato)
pic. 66 (Fabio Zonta)
pic. 78 (Franco Manfrotto).

Kind acknowledgements to the Libreria Palazzo Roberti for the following selections taken from the volume *Bassano nella memoria*, Bassano del Grappa 2001, *pic. 7, 9, 16, 25, 43, 47, 58, 77 (Archivio Fotografico Libreria Palazzo Roberti), pic. 107, 110, 120, 129-132.*

Index

A little, great, and effervescent city with an old heart, Bassano is both a hospitable and generous city. Rising from the mouth of the valley, at the top of a hill, it is protected by the barrier of the mountains, projected to the plain, and rocked by the river; it has always been at the cross roads of traffic and relations. Bassano's millennial history, documented with the acts of 998, is consolidated in the memory, and impressed in the stones and the character of its people. Rich in civilization, exquisitely Venetian, still bewitched by Serenissima, Bassano has been described as a delicate, suggestive, sweet and melanchonic, and lively and cosmopolitan city to be lived and loved by all.
Walking through its streets, taking in its perspectives, admiring its architecture, its monuments and squares, going down to the river Brenta, daydreaming on the wooden bridge (Ponte Vecchio) that joins the two banks, and soaking up the tastes and moods that Bassano is so generous and famous for, all brings happiness to one's life.
Bassano is also a city of arts and crafts and rich in culture; it offers museums, history, and innovatory vocations. The harmonious urban development is brought to life by the muses of opera and music, the ballet and theater, and an endless sequence of spectacular shows.
The present guide is easy to consult and concise, when it gives an account of the main features and most stimulating events as seen through paintings, prints, and photographs. This is a handy reference book that will stimulate and arouse further curiosity.
The first English edition of this guidebook comes out to coincide with another important event in this city, the exhibition dedicated to the great artist Antonio Canova, and to the genius and talent of his neoclassical sculptures. It will become a great travelling companion which will help you understand the city of Bassano and the surrounding areas. It will supply you with a wealth of information such as itineraries, interesting routes, tours, and dates that you will not want to miss. This guide will also give the visitor an opportunity to experience the heart and soul of this city and the surrounding areas through every sense and feeling, through emotions, suggestions, fragrances, taste, and architecture from all of Veneto that you will find every where that you look. Bassano is also included in the Hexagon Project, and is considered a pearl amongst pearls. All of this adds to the charm of this city, making it one of the most extraordinary, timeless, and unforgettable destinations in Italy.

Oscar Zago
President of V.I.P.

Luciano Fabris
Councillor of Tourism
Bassano del Grappa

From the Origins to the State of Veneto

A Name of Roman Origins

Bassano does not boast of very remote origins, in spite of its strategic position at the end of the Valsugana. The city was probably raised from the nucleus of an ancient agricultural farm.

The history of Bassano does not begin before the Roman age. Traces of ancient Venetic takeovers emerged near the city in San Giorgio di Angarano (burial ground) which today is called Motte and is located between Castion and Castel di Godego. Not even the names of places go back before the Roman domination, which must have started at the beginning of the first century b.C. Several roads of the historical center still today resume the course of the *centuriazione* (the division in Roman times of the land into "centuries") oriented in accordance with the outlines of the Padovan plan, rather than that of Vicenza, where the course of the Brenta established a natural border. It is from this organization of lands, concentrated in the hands of a few large estate owners, that subsequent villages derived their names. The endings *anus* and *ianus* (that we find in Bassano, Angarano, Cartigliano, etc.) indicate the great agricultural properties of the families (Bassius, Ancarius, and Cartilius). The villages developed around the internal court of the business administrative center. The remains of one of these villages have been traced to a locality on the right bank of the river Brenta, which was afterwards called Corte (Court). It is not easy to date the origin of spread of Christianity in the area but the first parishes were not recorded in documents before the 10th century. The churches often took the place of previous Roman temples, sometimes keeping the name (i.e. the church of San Vittore on the hill of Bassano, built on the place of the cult of the God Mitra, "winner" of evil).

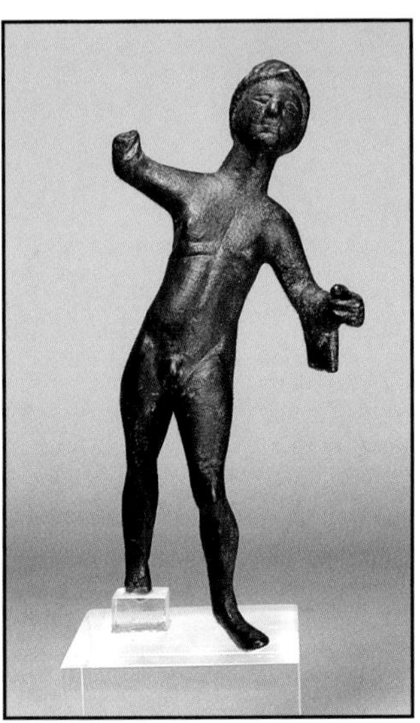

1-3. The Museum of Bassano has in its archeological department several protohistoric exhibits which come from the entire territory surrounding the city. Above next to the title, there is an antefix with the Gordon's head of the Augustan period from San Giorgio di Angarano. On the side you can see an attacking Hercules found at Cismon del Grappa (IV-I century B.C.). Below, a fibula in the form of pincers, from the Marchesane area. II-III century a.D.

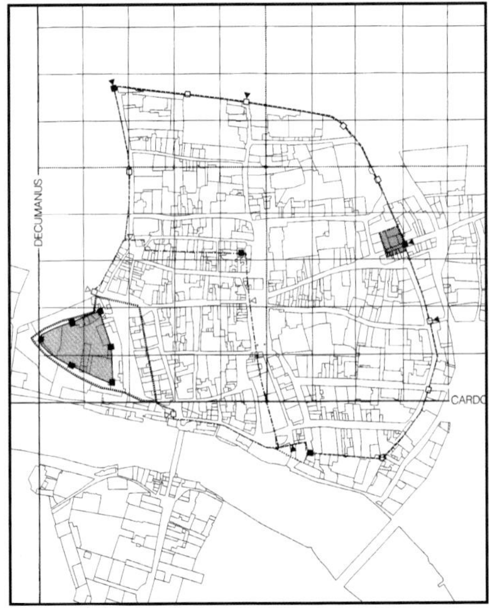

4. In Roman times the territory north of the Postumia Road was divided into "centuries", that is divided into a network of roads – from north to south (Cardines) *and from east to west* (Decumani) *– in a square grid with sides of about 700 m. The grid established at the same time the development of farm land, the road network and the city line of defense.*

THE *PLACITUM* OF 998: A DOCUMENT STILL WITHOUT A CITY

THE 1ST MILLENNIUM OF THE CHRISTIAN ERA PASSES AMONG INVASIONS, BATTLES, CHURCHES DEDICATED TO THE WARRIOR SAINTS. BASSANO DOES NOT EXIST YET, BUT THE PLACE IS A FATAL CROSSING. THE 2ND MILLENNIUM IS HISTORY.

The 22nd of July of 998 (a little more than a thousand years ago) «on the public road that is near the church of Santa Maria, a parish which is situated in Margnano and not far away from the river Brenta, Azeli, a messenger of the Emperor Ottone sat in the Court …». This is the beginning of the first document, a *placitum* (a decree), which states the official beginning of the history of Bassano. The city still does not exist, the notary public who wrote up the action found it sufficient to indicate the name of a church and the river but the place was Bassano. Since some years the city has celebrated this beginning with a choral show, *La Ballata del Millennio* (The Dance of the Millennium).

But the history of Bassano could have started before the millennium. Some names of places (Godego, Valgoda, and Godeluna) have gothic presence while others (Farra di Soligo, Fara Vicentina) attest, with the archaeological recoveries, a sequence of Lombard lookout-posts on the hills. The dedication to certain saints (like Donato or Giorgio) explains a diffused Lombard presence. The same can be said for the Francs. An important document by Berengario, before 915, gave the bishop of Padova the rights for some roads in the Bassano territory and also the authorization to erect a castle. But the first fortifications of the city most likely go back to after the bloody defeat of the troops of Berengario by the Hungarians, which happened a short distance from where the city would rise, between Nove and Cartigliano, on the river Brenta.

5. *In the picture, the ancient stone city coat-of-arms of the free borough of Bassano, formerly included on the ancient Gate of Lions, is now incorporated on the façade of the pawnbrokers in Piazzotto Montevecchio. The lions are the symbol of power while the gate-tower symbolizes the city.*

6. *The original of the placitum of 998 is lost. A later copy is conserved in Venice, in the Marciana library. The document was deliberated by a qualified assembly of bishops and counts from the delegation of the Venetian doge, and it testifies how the meeting point was strategic at the cross road of the communication between Treviso, Verona, Padova, and the north. It was not before 1147, and the Treaty of Peace between Padova and Vicenza, that Bassano was mentioned again as a town. Only in 1175 when the people from Bassano swore allegiance to Vicenza, the documents refer to a* castrum, *a castle, and to «suburbia sive burgos», the suburbs that had developed around the castle.*

A CASTLE OF CITIZENS

BETWEEN THE 12TH AND THE BEGINNING OF THE 13TH CENTURY THE FIRST NUCLEUS OF THE CITY IS DEFINED WITHIN THE TOWN-WALLS OVERLOOKED BY THE CASTLE, BRANCHING OFF TO THE NORTH (MARGNAN) AND TO THE SOUTH, WHERE THE BORGO LEON WILL GROW.

The oath of fidelity to Vicenza (1175) signals for the first time the existence of a castle and a village, but also the fact that they were governed by free men, not subject to the power of the nobles, but only to the far dependency of the royal power. Therefore it is evident that Bassano did not rise from a feudal stronghold and that the hill on which the parish of Santa Maria was built was fortified by its citizens. This has also been proved by the original position of the buildings to the inside of the *castrum*, with examples being the *canipe* (the modest buildings in wood in which agricultural and other products were safely stored), the first *domus comunis* (communal buildings) between the parish and the church of San Vittore, and the cemetery (which was transferred only in 1822). After many centuries it is difficult to exactly perceive the first stratifications of the castle. The structure was polygonal (but looked like a triangle) and did not have foundations, the walls created a double fencing and there were no protruding towers so it was protected along the curtain. The defensive structure was protected by a slope which was dominated by the observation tower, in a diagonal position with reference to the walls of Sir Ivano (the name of the head chief of an armed band at the service of the Ezzelini). Opposite there was the esplanade of Terraglio that in ancient times was delimited by an open gallery with workshops. The role of the castle, important for the urban development of the city, is still prominent and evident. The first circle of walls sprouting from the castle was

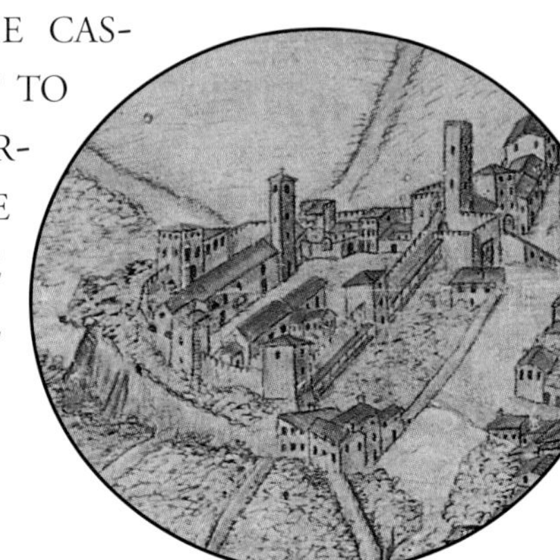

▲ *7-8. Above a detail of the map of Bassano by Francesco and Leandro dal Ponte which represents the area of the castle. The drawing shows a bird's eye view of Bassano. It was realized between 1583 and 1610 and it is conserved in the Museum of Bassano in the map archives. Here below is a partial view of the same area.* ▼

▲ *9-10. In a photograph from 1853, the ancient walls of the castle with the Fontico and the Tower of Sir Ivano from the Terraglio esplanade. Below, a charming view of the tower of Sir Ivano: from the 13th century, built diagonally from the wall, it shows the architectural device adopted in Ezzelinian times to build corner flankers in fortifications.* ▼

built within the first decades of the 13th century. Clockwork wise, employing the names of the roads as seen today, the plan of the city developed to the east towards Piazzetta Zaine continuing to the south through the Vendramini alley and from there going west towards the present Palazzo Sturm. Then it ran along the upper margins of the public squares Garibaldi and Libertà and of Via Portici Lunghi. From there it ascended along the river going beyond the bridge on the Brenta, towards the Callesello dell'Orco, and as far as the castle. This, together with the small fortress of Porto di Brenta, had a vice like control of the bridge on the water way. The walls featured four gates, the most important being Porta di Margnano to the north and the only one still partly visible, Porta dell'Aureola or di Oriente on Piazzotto Zaine, and Porta dei Leoni to the south, each enclosed in an impressive *zirone* (tower). There were also two small gates today only partially visible, with locks and draw bridges, posterns, and towers on the bank of the river to defend the bridge. Outside the walls an embankment with thorn hedges and duplicate ditches filled up with rain water. Inside, the town plan in spite of the slope of the land, resumed the Roman grid system. The houses with inner courtyards lined up along the perimeter ended with open galleries. Two axis determined the layout of the village. The first from the Castle gate to the Porta dei Leoni, where the road to Padova started; the second, from the bridge to the Porta dell'Aureola, defined the median zone of the town.

The Emperor Offers a Rose

THE DOMINION OF THE EZZELINI DID NOT BRING ABOUT SUDDEN CHANGES IN THE URBAN PATTERN, BUT IT STRENGHTENED THE CITIZENS OF BASSANO'S FEELING TOWARDS FREEDOM, ENHANCING THEIR CIVIL UNITY. AND IT LEFT BEHIND SOME UNEXPECTED TRACES...

The castle and the first walled settlement of the city arose from a *communitas* (commune) of freemen who were not subject to any explicit feudal bond. But in the late 12th century the clear influence of the da Romano family of Bassano who owned property in town and in the surrounding areas, soon changed to accomplished rule. In 1259, the year of the fall of Ezzelino III the Tyrant, 186 buildings were confiscated from the family. Their economic power, which made the village such a strategic location and a perfect base for steady expansion, (at the peak of their power the family controlled the whole of Veneto from Verona to Treviso), soon entitled them to permanent rights. In 1218 the rector of the monastery of San Benedetto in Padova acknowledged in an arbitrator's award, the co-existence in Basssano of the prerogatives of both the municipal administration of Vicenza and of the da Romano family.
Over 20 years earlier, Ezzelino II in urgent need of a large amount of money had offered to yield the city to Padova although he did not have the authority to do so. However, the darkest period of submission was registered between 1223-1259, when Ezzelino III, who was known as one of the most ambitious, unscrupulous, and cruel masters of his time, ruled as the powerful imperial vicar of Federico II for the city of Treviso. Bassano was his loyal supporter until his downfall. Despite his power, Ezzelino did not make his mark on the city. His family did contribute to the construction of the town walls by improving

11-13. Next to the title the genealogical coat-of-arms of the da Romano family. In the other two pictures the frescos that are dated around 1239 in Palazzo Finco. Here is a beautifully painted Troubador scene, which shows when compared to other portraits of the sovereign one of the most realistic and fascinating portraits of Federico II, caught in the act of offering a rose to a lady of royal rank. This was quite unusual to the imperial protocol. One of the two mysterious characters in the portrait, who is next to Federico, could even be Alberico da Romano.

the fortifications, which were partly built after the 1228 siege by the Padovani, and set the basis for the later development of the village. However it is merely a legend that ascribes to him the erection of the great tower on the square, whose role in the town will be talked about further on. Moreover, Bassano never granted him the unconditional dominion of the castle where he owned a *canipa* (cellar) as many others did, and also a *palacium* (administration office).

The issue of the exact identification of the two *domus super plateam* (houses in the square) which were later confiscated is debatable. The houses used to be on the square that was characterized by the well, or square of the town hall, is today known as Piazzotto Montevecchio. A portion of the buildings, belonging to Alberico (Ezzelino's brother) can be traced in part to the present day Palazzo Finco in Via Zaccaria Bricito, 26-30, where in the process of a restoration in 1992 an extraordinary fresco came to light. Although it does not seem that Bassano's town-planning was upset by the Ezzelinian rule; it is undeniable that they guaranteed the growth of the town through updated cultural and artistic trends. Bassano was also strengthened by the contribution of their army, who after the tyrant's fall, were able to gather and fully join in communal life.

▲ ▶ *14-16. In the center an incision from the end of the 16th century, by Aliprando Caprioli from Trieste, which comes from the Collection Remondini in the Museum of Bassano, showing the terrible Ezzelino III da Romano. Above in a modern shot and below in a picture from the beginning of the early 20th century Piazzoto Montevecchio. This is the oldest square in the city, formally known as* Platea a puteo, *because of the main well that provided water for the city and was closed in 1568.* ▼

A NEW AXIS, A "TORRE GRANDA"

BETWEEN THE 13TH AND 14TH CENTURY THE TOWN PLANNING DOUBLES, PROTECTED BY THE NEW SURROUNDING WALL. THE NEW ORDER OF THE CITY DEFINES A PRIVILEGED AXIS CONNECTING ANCIENT AND MODERN FORTIFICATIONS, TOWERS, AND CENTERS OF POWER.

With the defeat of Ezzelino (1259), the town of Bassano had reconquered its independence, but it was one that was not meant to last. A year later the town was controlled by Vicenza, then in 1267 it returned under the power of Padova who ruled with wisdom until 1320 when the Scaligeri (Dalla Scala family from Verona) took over, and then once again Padova ruled, followed by the Visconti until to the Serenissima government. Such rapid changes of hands were unlikely to realize any dramatic urban development or changes. There was only a gradual growth of the city, which was managed by the cities magistrate and endorsed by the succeeding dominions. The most relevant role was largely plaid by the Padovani.
The influence of the town council is to be found in regulations established by successive by-laws in 1259, 1295, and 1389 (the defense of the town by fortifying the outer villages which rose around the main walled nucleus, the prevention of fires by means of roofs made of tiles instead of straw, and the prohibition of excessive housing concentration). In the communal age, the city knew a continuous development that forced house construction outside the walls of the original crowded settlement. This created the premise for the construction of the outer circle of walls which coincides today with the historic center of Bassano. It is more inter-

17-18. The legend attributes the Tower of the Piazza (here below in a modern shot) to Ezzelino, but it was actually started by the Padovani around 1315 and it was completed after their reign. As shown in The map of Bassano *from 1690-1691 (on the left) the Tower used to be in the center of the town at an equal distance between the two castles. This made it possible to shoot crossbows in the direction of both the old and new town gates. The Tower was built out of pebbles covered with limestone slabs on a base in the shape of a truncated pyramid. It was higher (40 m. high and 14 m. wide) than the San Francesco complex, enough to be an observation point of advantage to monitor what was taking place within or at the border of the city. Throughout the centuries both restorations and additions were made: the clock is dated from 1746 and the battlements from 1823 by Antonio Gaidon.*

esting to reflect on the way in which the new perimeter was oriented than on its dimensions. The essential axis of the development reverted to Via Nova (today known as Via Roma) and then continued into Via Beata Giovanna and beyond. This interrupted the standard formulation of the ancient *centuriatio* addressing itself diagonally and in a perfect straight road towards Padova. It is not only this evident connection between the controlled Bassano and the dominating city of Padova that characterizes the new axis. It was also connected perfectly to the gate of the ancient higher Castle, through the Contrada del Palazzo (today Via Matteotti). It received its name from the Cassero de la Torre Bianca (later Palazzo Pretorio) and was built up by the Padovani in 1315 as the headquarters for the Podestà and the captains, abandoning the previous positioning in the Piazza del Pozzo (later Piazzotto Montevecchio).
The construction of the Lower Castle, in the center of the southern margin of the new tracing of the walls, next to a second gate (Porta dei Leoni), reveals the explicit intentions of the new rulers to unify along the same axis the defense functions of the town, the political representation, the customs offices, and all social aspects.

▲ 19-23. Above to your left a view of the tower seen from the church of San Francesco and to the right the Franciscan complex of buildings observed from the ogival windows of the Torre Granda. Here below an aerial picture of the town: at the center of the picture you can recognize the 14th century Via Nova axis (today Via Roma), also pictured below in the previous page in an anonymous map of the city from 1760-1767. Under the text to the right there is a view of the Palazzo Pretorio, facing the ancient Contrada del Palazzo (today Via Matteotti). ▼

The Central Squares

THE NEW CIRCLE OF WALLS RESHAPES THE INNER TOWN PLANNING. IN THE CENTER, TWO LONGITUDINAL PUBLIC SQUARES BEGIN TO DEFINE THEMSELVES IN SUCCESSION, DESTINED TO BE FROM THEN ON THE TRUE CENTER OF BASSANO. THE ROLE OF THE CHURCH OF SAN FRANCESCO.

The new 13th and 14th century circle of defense walls made use of the natural environment. To the west, the southern extension of the curtain followed the course of the river Brenta at a wider distance from the bank. To the northeast, good use was made of alluvial terrace, facing the field of Santa Caterina. From these two fixed lines the continuation of planning was designed starting from where today is Piazzale Trento. In regular intervals there were towers that held into account the changing defensive needs of the town. To the inside, new zones joined together according to a longitudinal pattern from north to south leaving obvious traces today in the road system that assumes a rectangular shape (see the long crossroads of Via Museo, Via Marinali, Via Verci, Via Campo Marzio, with in the middle Via Nova, today known as Via Roma). The new gates that were opened in the more external strip, corresponded roughly to the previous scanning, and were determined by the roads that radiated from the center of the city. The median transverse axis was traced from Porto di Brenta to as far as the segment of the wall, where at the beginning of the 17th century the Portello dei

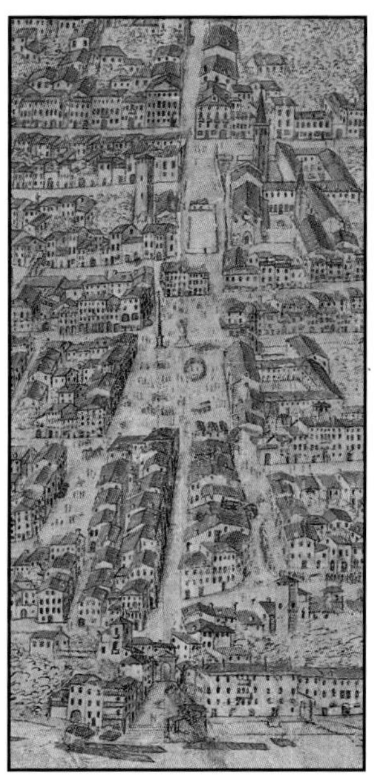

▲ *24-27. Next to the title is the incision by Alessandro Dalla Via with the solemn procession for the communion of the sick (1700). Here above, left a detail of the* Map of Bassano *by Francesco Leandro dal Ponte with the road axis that crosses the new squares of the city. Above, right there is a view of Piazza Garibaldi and below there is a view of Piazza Libertà.* ▼

28-29. *On the southern side of the two squares, in a position of importance for the development of the new urban network, two of the most important religious buildings of Bassano were built: the church of San Francesco (above, to the right; below the interior) and the Oratory and the hospital of San Giovanni Battista (here above), destined to undergo profound modifications over the course of the following centuries.*

Riformati would be opened. Therefore Via Portici led to an elongated public square that was divided into two spaces (Invaso di San Giovanni and Invaso di San Francesco), and continued down Contrada Rigorba, today known as Via Jacopo dal Ponte. As it has been noticed by scholars, this public square, destined to become the main one of Bassano (with the names today of Piazza Libertà and Piazza Garibaldi), resumes typologies that are to be found both in the alpine areas, Austria, and in the Italian examples (L'Aquila, Brescia, with the ancient market square).

30. *The Franciscan Church, where the friar minors moved from the previous monastery of San Donato di Angarano (officiated in 1227), was built between the last decade of the 13th century and 1331 and was dedicated to the founder of the order. The external still conserves along the nave the original lines of the brickwork and the river pebbles of the walls with brickwork pilaster strips joined under the eaves by blind pointed arches. The façade is made beautiful by the rose window, and amongst 14th century tombs, by an elegant protiro with pointed arches attributed to Boninsegna di Bellino by an inscription over the portal. During the 14th century the interior of the nave was extensively frescoed, although only few later traces remain after the baroque transformations, such as an enormous St. Christopher on the south side of the church. On the far side of choir the Holy Cross from the church of Santa Maria in Colle which was made by Guariento during the late phase of his maturity, is very striking. The artist had already made shortly after 1332 for the church of San Francesco his juvenile master piece, the big cross now preserved in the city Museum located in the Franciscan monastery.*

Erba che produce Rorate
lago di bottiro fresco
O che Macharoni
Prigioni
per chi li
lauorare
le Vache in questo paese ogni
mese partoriscono li Vitelli
lago di fritele
non si pensa
non che a
alegri
qui li Canoni
gieta fiaschi
di moscato
Questo e il
il piu Pol

The Civilization of Images

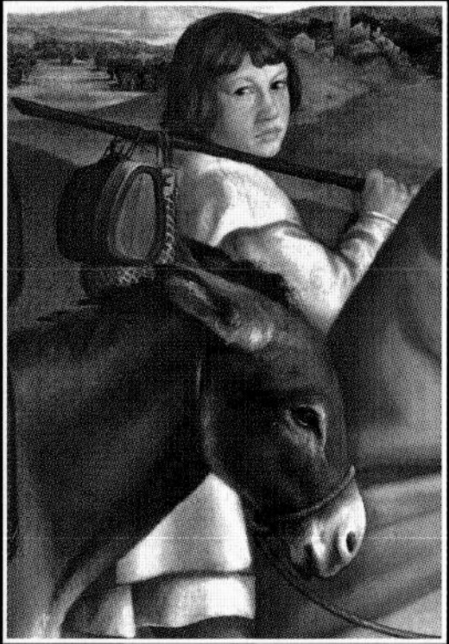

The Venetian Dominion: the City as a Monument

The government of Serenissima did not dramatically change the urban planning of Bassano but it only added some important monuments (such as the Loggia di Piazza) and generally improved the buildings.

On the 10th of June 1404 the first Venetian troops made their entrance in Bassano. The Serenissima had strategically exploited the conflict between the Visconti and the lords of Padova. The dedication of the citizens was pacific and their fidelity to the new lords guaranteed the defense of the village and the respect of its statutes, supplying reassuring economic perspectives, and freeing the people from the near dependencies of Padova and Vicenza.

The new political situation that would last until the end of the 18th century, did not determine dramatic changes in the shape of the town that by then had taken its definition. The tracing of the walls was not changed, but only periodically restored. At the beginning of the 16th century, a Loggia which was a lookout in order to admire the panorama, was built outside of the Porta delle Grazie. This was one of the first signs of the will to make the accesses to the city more monumental. The Loggia would later become a measure of comparison with the gate of Castello Inferiore (which still bears the name of Dieda from the Podestà who was the curator of the restoration) and with Porta di Margnano, Porta delle Grazie, and Porta di Brenta.

From this perspective we can also include the Loggia di Piazza, or del Comune, started in 1405, in the crucial area of the division between Piazza San Giovanni (now Piazza della Libertà) and Piazza San Francesco (now Garibaldi). Initially on the ground floor, with arches along the south and the west sides, it was equipped with a clock by Corrado da Feltre that since

▲ *31-33. Left, the fresco by Francesco Bassano il Vecchio,* San Christopher *on the façade of the Loggia di Piazza. Below a view of the pawnbrokers (Monte di Pietà) and the tempera on canvas (1906) by Gaspare Fontana (Bassano 1871-1943) with the reproduction of the façade of the tower of Porta Dieda.* ▼

1430 symbolized the flowing of secular time in the city. The Loggia was expanded vertically in the course of the 15th century, and conveniently restored after the destruction caused by the war of the League of Cambrai. The present appearance of the Loggia is the same as the one of 1582, when the 15th century clock was replaced with the one by Giovanni dal Molino from Asiago, while the one seen today is by the important 18th century engineer Bartolomeo Ferracina from Bassano. Some frescos by Jacopo Bassano survived (many destroyed in a fire in 1682), and still decorate the façade today, while inside you can see the 120 coats-of-arms of the first Venetian Podestà. The construction of the Loggia must have corresponded with that of the buildings, amongst which the most striking is Casa Cataruzzi-Danieli, that still separate, without modifications, the two public squares.

Another area considerably modified and characterized in the Venetian age, before the construction of the Loggia on the north side of Piazza San Giovanni, is that of Piazzotto Montevecchio. Already in the 14th century, the *domus comunis* had been transferred by the Padovani to the Cassero della Torre Bianca, later to become Palazzo Pretorio. On the ancient site of Maggior Consiglio was most likely built the Fontego dei Grani, and then from 1492 the Monte di Pietà (the pawnbrokers), that will give the ultimate name to the Slargo. On the eastern side of the square there were rows of high quality housing, amongst which we find the Casa dal Corno, which was entirely frescoed by Jacopo Bassano.

▲ ▶ *34-35. Right, the small fresco of* The Virgin *by Jacopo dal Ponte inserted in the front of the Loggia di Piazza. The building above was started in 1405 and the last restoration was completed in 1582.*

The Painted City

The passage from medieval building to modern building also favors the decoration of the façades of the houses and according to a Venetian custom that here, especially after the intervention by Jacopo dal Ponte, obtained a particularly high quality.

The transformation of building practices from wooden structures to those exclusively in masonry is to be ascribed to the Venetian dominion. This progressive change is attested with certain evidence by a group of buildings along the upper part of Via Matteotti, at the crossing of Via Gamba and the continuation into Via Bonamigo in the immediate vicinity of Porta del Castello. In this area, the Casa Bonamigo al Terraglio, with its mythological decorations on the upper part of the façade, demonstrates with sufficient clarity the transition from the mode of medieval building to that of the Renaissance.

With very few exceptions, Bassano does not assimilate the architectonic Venetian inclinations of the age (the late gothic period), instead showing a clear preference for those more compact and sober that were typical of the mainland. These buildings were better suited to have frescoed exteriors, a diffused characteristic that we see throughout the city of Bassano.

The frescoed town, with

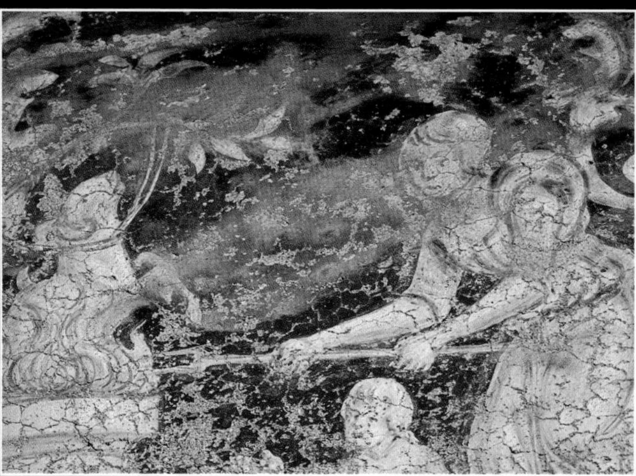

36-37. Right, a detail of a mythological scene of the fresco decorations (1497) of Casa Bonamigo, in the road of the same name (# 29-30), here below.

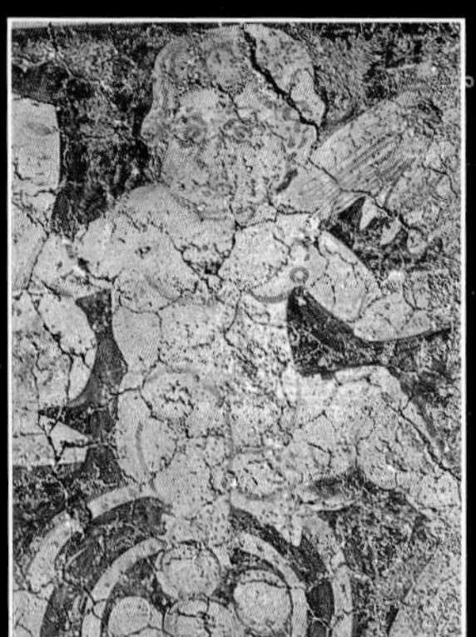

38. Left, another particular frescoed surface of the Casa Bonamigo: the humanist Lazzaro who commissioned the work, also conceived the idea for the fresco (1497) which was inspired by the ancient vase paintings.

▲ *39. Francesco and Bartolomeo Nasocchi, a particular of the frescoed decoration in the Casa Michieli (1539) in Piazza Libertà: the frieze with cupids surrounds the panels with the* Story of the Hebrew Joseph.

some examples at the margins of the city (like Ca' Erizzo) prevailed particularly in the 15th and 16th centuries, before allowing the more durable gravity of memorial and marble stones, and classical taste less inclined to colors (excluding nineteenth century alterations) to take over. The first examples with geometrical patterns such as the passage to sacred images (not to be confused with properly named shrines) and the mythological scenes (sometimes combined with the sacred ones, as expressed in the decoration of Casa Treviso in Vicolo Vittorelli) advanced quite rapidly. It ended up providing workmen from Bassano to the Nasocchi workshops (to whom the intervention of Casa Michieli, on the eastern side of Piazzotto Montevecchio can be attributed) and also to the workshops of Jacopo dal Ponte.

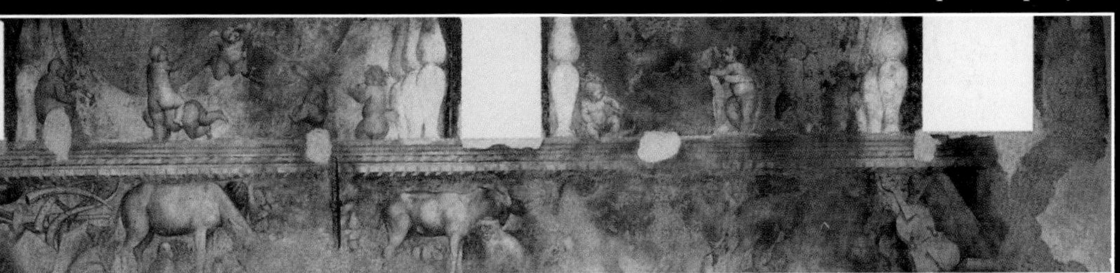

▲ *40-41. Above, the frescoes of Casa dal Corno, unfortunately are the only ones to have survived the course of time. Amongst the numerous documented interventions are those by Jacopo dal Ponte which were returned to the city Museum for conservation. from above images of cupids, animals amongst cultural symbols, allegroes, and biblical scenes from the old testament. It is a complex whole with additions of extraodinary realism.* ▶

▲ *42. A particular section of the frescos on the façade of Casa Marcon in Piazzetta dell'Angelo: these were painted in the second half of the XVI century by an anonymous artist who was not from Bassano, and show mythological gods enclosed within a* tromp-l'oeil *architectural frame.*

Ponte Vecchio, the Old Bridge

The symbol of the city on the shore of the river, a belowed subject by 18th century painters, the bridge was also a permanent laboratory for architectonic and technological solutions. The main protagonists were Palladio and Ferracina.

The first documents handed down to us regarding the bridge of Bassano, a secular symbol of the city, date back to the year 1209, when the notary public Gerardo Maurisio informs of a curious act of public submission to Ezzelino. Even so the construction of the bridge was considered more ancient. The importance of the structure, raised where the banks of the river Brenta narrowed, was essential, in that it favored the communication between the territories of Treviso and Vicenza. It started from the village of Angarano on the right bank, which would conserve an administrative autonomy from Bassano until 1812.

A symbol of the city, a crossing between various civilizations, the bridge was often exposed to the fury of the river, (the terrible *brentana*) and together with the events of war was destroyed repeatedly. It was frequently rebuilt («patient construction», Lionello Puppi wrote) over the course of time as a sign of its own memory. The first edification of the town-walls of the city revolved as we have seen around the position of the bridge. Although we do not have credible iconographic documentation on the medieval shape of the bridge as far as the number of pylons and the aspect of the cover, it was almost certainly built in wood, according to alpine standards, given to the great availability of lumber and the greater elasticity of this on stone. But it is presumable that, through the course of the centuries, a

▲ *43-45. Next to the title a part of the map of Bassano by Francesco e Leandro dal Ponte. Throughout the centuries the bridge connecting the city to the village of Angarano has become the shining symbol of the town of Bassano.*

▲ 46. Il Ponte di Bassano *(The Bridge of Bassano), 1807, by Roberto Roberti (Bassano 1786-1837) located in the Museum of Bassano.*

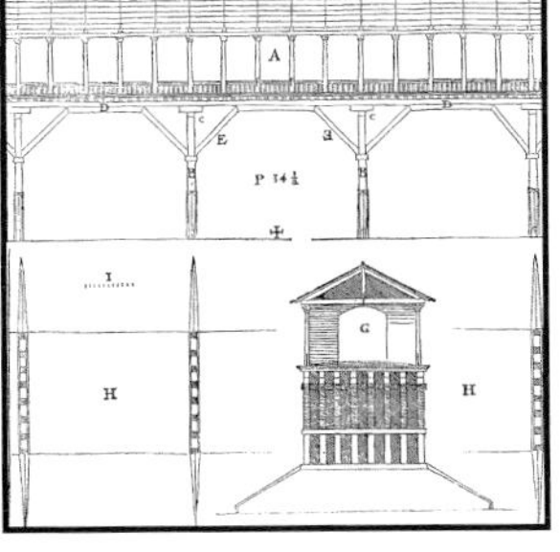

▲ ▼ *47-50. The bridge (here in two different views, one from the inside and one within the city), was destroyed several times (in 1450, 1493, 1511, 1520, 1524, 1526, 1567, 1748, 1813, and 1945): the last reconstruction was promoted by the National Association of Alpini. Here above is an architectural sketch from* Quattro Libri *(Four Books) by Palladio with his plan for the bridge.*

precise tradition developed involving local and qualified craftsmen.

It is only in the course of the 16th century that foremen from Chiavenna, Padova and Cremona were brought to Bassano with disastrous results. This was until the involvement, after the collapse of 1567, of one of the greatest Venetian architects of the time, Andrea Palladio, who in his treaty, edited in Venice a few years later, provided a long description and a precise design of his "invention". Palladio, without indulging in the taste that he had used for the plan of the Venetian bridge of Rialto, also tries here to suggest using the shapes of the arches for the support («These beams arranged in this manner communicate the aspect of an arch», he wrote). For the walkway he proposed an elegant enclosed Loggia, destined, with some variations, to being preserved forever. The 16th and 17th century prints show to us sufficiently the Palladian solution. It lasted for nearly two centuries, until the frightful flood of 1748, when the bridge was reconstructed by *fabro oriolajo*, the hydraulic expert Bartolomeo Ferracina. Although during the full swing of the neo-Palladian era many people supported the importance to imitate the 16th century *exemplum*, he pragmatically proposed a more rational alternative. It was not until the last adaptation of the bridge (but not the cover) that we saw the Palladian ideas reasserted by Casarotti in 1821.

In the bridge as it is today we can see the synthesis of the 16th and 18th century plans, which are celebrated by many paintings of the 19th century.

GENIUS LOCI

IN A CITY WITHOUT FIGURATIVE TRADITION IN THE 16TH CENTURY, THE TALENT AND THE COMPLEX PERSONALITY OF JACOPO DAL PONTE EXPLODES ONTO THE ART SCENE. HE WAS ONE OF THE GREAT MASTERS OF VENETO IN THE CENTURY AND THE SUCCESS OF HIS WORKS WAS IMMENSE.

Although being a rich and civil center, Bassano did not have until the 16th century an independent artistic tradition. It comes to no surprise that the genius who redeemed the situation had the same name of the city. Jacopo (1510/15-1592) was the son of a painter of limited horizons, the elder Francesco Bassano, and grandson of a tanner from Asiago, who foresaw the role that a valued artist could carry out in the village at the foot of Mount Grappa. In many documents he is called Jacopo dal Ponte. In fact a legend says that his studio overlooked the river Brenta and the bridge, while it was actually in Salita Ferracina. He was sent by Francesco to Venice to be trained in the bottega of Bonifacio de' Pitati. Then, apart from short intervals in his later years, he always developed his research in Bassano. He turned out to be one of greatest protagonists of the golden century of Venetian painting.

In spite of some recurrent themes (the extreme attention for the natural reality and the scenes of daily life, the studies of the role of light in painting, an amazing ability to interpret religious topics through daily life) his style changed many times. This confirmed an incredible curiosity for the studies of art practiced in his time and his inexhaustible desire to experiment. His first biographers wrote about his four "periods" (modern students of art have expanded the number

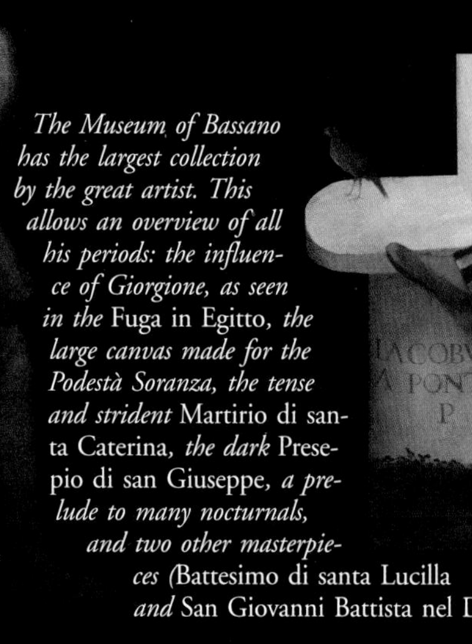

The Museum of Bassano has the largest collection by the great artist. This allows an overview of all his periods: the influence of Giorgione, as seen in the Fuga in Egitto, *the large canvas made for the Podestà Soranza, the tense and strident* Martirio di santa Caterina, *the dark* Presepio di san Giuseppe, *a prelude to many nocturnals, and two other masterpieces (*Battesimo di santa Lucilla *and* San Giovanni Battista nel Deserto.*)*

of these phases) in which the lessons of Giorgione and Roman art are clearly visible, along with the mannerism of central Italy and the Nordic taste for the details, chromatic elegance and formal wisdom.
He was greatly admired by Tiziano, who accommodated him many times in Venice. Italian collectors and collectors from the north of Europe disputed over his small landscapes and Biblical scenes from peasant life. From a very young age he never lacked commissions by the Venetian Podestà and by the church. In the middle of the 17th century Giambattista Tiepolo, in a famous letter to his son, emphasized the perfection of his art. The most prestigious opportunities were offered to him in Bassano. Though various works of his, most especially exterior frescos, have been lost through the years, the Museum of Bassano dedicates to him a substantial itinerary of all the stages of his works. Anticipating the genre painting of 17th century taste and the new rules of the art market (the small formats and the scenes in sequence) Jacopo Bassano, a master at drawing, did not find in his children the heir to develop further his work, despite the unexpected success on the Venetian scene of his elder son, Francesco il Giovane. Even after Jacopo Bassano's death, the story of Bassano was permeated with the suggestion of images, colors, and the values attributed to artistic practice.

The City, Places of Devotion and a Patron Saint

With the exception of the area of the castle, the strongest urban role was exercised by the churches of San Francesco and San Giovanni Battista, the greatest amongst all of the religious buildings. The reasons of the cult of San Bassiano.

Apart from the important 14th century church of San Francesco, Bassano does not boast of any other extraordinary religious buildings. Although many ancient buildings have endured over the course of the centuries radical restructuring (most especially in the baroque age) they lost numerous frescos and other precious decorations. Most of these had been destroyed during the Napoleonic suppressions at the beginning of the 19th century, though fortunately part of the pictorial furnishings had been stored in the storage rooms of the city Museum.

It could be useful to regroup the most significant ones in a synthetic itinerary that points out above all the urban value of the various dislocations. As we know, the cathedral of the city, Pieve di Santa Maria in Colle, to the inside of the Castello Superiore, precedes the first official document of the history of Bassano. Though there are not any finds from before the year 1000 retraceable *in situ*, a wooden crucifix of the 12th century is now placed in the church of San Francesco, while there have recently emerged traces of 13th century frescos of good quality, over the door to the east of the southern flank. Enlarged several times from 1471, the interior of the church defines itself at the end of the 17th century with a great rectangular hall, adorned with giant pilaster strips along the walls, an apsis flanked by two chapels, and canvases by Giovanni Volpato on the ceiling.

▲ *57-60. Next to the title is the late 13th century anonymous frescos from Santa Maria in Colle. Here above, the external part of the church and a detail of* The Map of Bassano *by Francesco and Leandro dal Ponte with the complex of Santa Caterina, today partly missing. Below, the interior of the cathedral after the baroque transformation.*

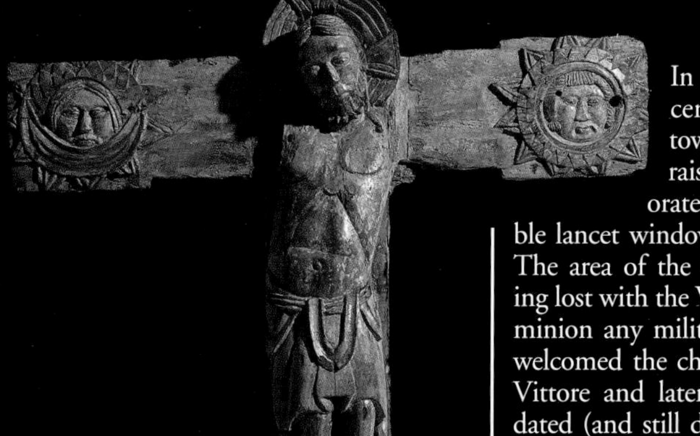

In 1733 a 13th century bell tower was also raised and decorated with double lancet windows.

The area of the Castle, having lost with the Venetian dominion any military valence, welcomed the church of San Vittore and later accommodated (and still does) the oratory of San Filippo Neri, transformed in 1810 in the School of Design.

Many religious buildings are situated outside of walls, or along them. To the north, in the area of Margnano we find the convent of San Sebastiano that was built on a preexisting Lombard base, by the 11
hermits of Pietro Malerba, then by the Agostinian nuns, and finally by the Capuchin friars. Some fragments of frescos testify to the remote origins of the takeover and a small portion survived from the church and the hostel of Santa Caterina. To the east, the church of San Bonaventura of the Riformati, dated at the beginning of the 17th century and later included in the first Bassano hospital, determined the opening in the walls of the homonymous gate to the beginning of the road of what today is called Via Jacopo dal Ponte. To the south, on the axis of Via Nova, the church of the Sacred Heart was founded on the late 15th century San Girolamo for which young Jacopo Bassano painted the *Escape into Egypt*, today in the city Museum), and

▲ *61-62. Above on the left, a picture of the internal of the Franciscan church of San Donato at Angarano, the first settlement of the order in the city. On the right a picture of the large wooden crucifix from the 12th century, which was once located in the church of Santa Maria in Colle but is now located in the church of San Francesco. The Christ has lost his arms, but the arms of the crucifix still hold the symbols of the sun and the moon which is a northern tradition.*

▲ *63-65. Above on the left is the façade of the late 15th century church of Santa Maria delle Grazie, and on the right the remains of the frescos. To the right one of the few traces left of the fresco decoration in the internal of the church of San Francesco.* ▶

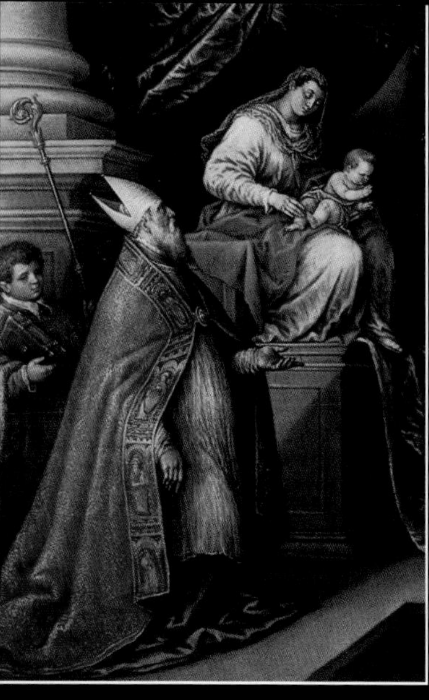

the church of Santa Maria della Misericordia, or della Beata Giovanna, now in a 17th century style, but built on a preexisting building from 1390. To the west, beyond the Ponte Vecchio, the ancient Franciscan church of San Donato.

Amongst the buildings the bulk of Santa Maria delle Grazie dated towards the end of the 15th century stands out along the walls. It is still very well preserved inside, with a 15th century canopy and frescos by Battista da Vicenza, Nasocchi and Jacopo dal Ponte.

Much different is the urban role of the church of San Giovanni Battista dated from the beginning of the 14th century, on the southern side of the Piazza della Libertà, opposite the long row of houses with a continuous lower open gallery. The present aspect, in three parts, was defined in the course of 17th centu-

▲ *66-68. Above on the left a detail of the painting by Leandro dal Ponte from 1590 commissioned by Podestà Lorenzo Cappello: at the foot of the throne of the Virgin, garbed in bishop's clothing, the figure of San Bassiano, protector of the city. On the right, a view of the statue of the saint protector located in Piazza Libertà, by Orazio Marinali (1682). Here below, the recent restoration of the statue of the blessed Giovanna Maria Bonomo (Asiago 1606 - Bassano 1670), by the sculptor Felice Chiereghini from Padova (1784). Giovanna Maria (blessed in June 9, 1783) spent an exemplary life marked by miracles and supernatural apparitions in the Benedictine convent of San Girolamo. She was nominated for patron and protector of the city, spared during the invasion by Napoleon in January 1799. When the convent was incorporated in to state property at the beginning of the 19th century, her remains and the cult where transferred to the church of Santa Maria* ◀ *della Misericordia.*

69-70. During the 18th century the architect Giovanni Miazzi assembled inside of the church of San Giovanni three areas in longitudinal sequence according to an unusual liturgical axis of orientation, perpendicular to the square; the one to the east is one of the most refined expressions of rococo from Basssano. This is the chapel of SS. Sacramento with stuccos by the Lombard artists Abbondio Stazio and Carpoforo Mazzetti. The central hall is very short indeed, consequently giving the impression that the ceiling is very high, and is decorated with frescos by the painter Giovanni Scajario in style of Tiepolo. Right, the plan for the altar by Orazio Marinali and below an overall picture.

ry. A short distance from the church of San Giovanni, in Via Marinali, you notice the 15th century hospital of San Paolo, built for the assistance of the poor and travelers.

In the western side of Piazza della Libertà, on a stone base, the statue of San Bassiano, the city patron, carved in 1682 by Orazio Marinali stands out. The Bishop of Lodi between the 4th and 5th centuries revealed himself to be a most effective safeguard from the most ferocious epidemics. The choice could have fallen on this saint, according to established customs, in order to gratify the identity of the city, with the plain resumption of his name. In effect, as recent studies have proved, it would not have been a matter of an accurate search of an eponym, but rather the suggestion of the hermit Friar Antonio, son of a German furrier, who had been born in Bassano, and abandoned the paternal activity following a disease in 1494, when he dedicated himself to prayer in the abandoned church of San Vito, just outside the walls of the city (where, some decades later, Ignazio da Loyola himself paid him a visit). It would have been him that promoted amongst his fellow citizens the cult of the old Bishop of Lodi, a cult that some documents attest to have been already operating most probably thanks to some Lombards who immigrated to Veneto at the end of the 13th century, which was the time of the reign of the Visconti.

The City Palaces

The monumental aspect of the city established itself first in the 16th and then in 18th centuries. Choices were made for sober elegance without affectations, but also without sparing the decoration of the interiors.

The urban aspect of the city is defined, almost completely in a span of time comprised between the 16th and 18th centuries. The map by Francesco and Leandro dal Ponte supplies the first general view towards 1610, of a situation that will find its apex at the beginning of the great plague of 1631. Within the consolidated urban plan, where the functions of the medieval defensive machine are gradually given up, some buildings of particular interest stand out. They were regular palaces, although like the churches, none of them really emerge glamorously.
What is possible to perceive is a general tone in the style of the buildings, although rich in variety, they all tended to lean towards a sober *décor.* Fernando Rigon wrote «the style of the façades with a minimum chromatic contrast, combines hues in which the use of brick red prevails for the backgrounds and the markings, perhaps a reminder of the color of the marble of Asiago». After the splendor of the painted city, what research is now about is «a style of string-courses and plain underlining of the framework and of windows. The smooth walls were denied every possibility of fresco enrichment, in a way to induce research for the true quality and beauty inside the buildings...». Among early examples of interior frescos the most striking is most certainly to be found in Palazzo Pretorio, with interventions from the 15th century. However, the interior frescos found their expressive apex between the18th and 19th century (some very good example are the Remondini houses along Piazza Libertà, the

▲ *71-73. In the background of the page is* The Map of Bassano *by Francesco and Leandro dal Ponte. Here above the Palazzo del Tribunale (the court house), once owned by the Antonibon family. Below to the left is a view of Via Jacopo dal Ponte with façades of Palazzo Lugo and Palazzo Compostella. On the right the late 16th century façade of Palazzo Brocchi along the homonymous slope.* ▼

Palazzo Roberti in Via dal Ponte, and Palazzo Sturm in Via Ferracina).

But regarding the external aspect of the Bassano palaces we can distinguish the more considerable buildings of the 16th century from those that were defined over the course of the 18th century. The first phase of the transformation of Bassano into a city of monuments corresponded with the building of 15th century Palazzo Cappello Manardi along Via Campo Marzio and on the parallel road (today Via Verci), the more recent Palazzo Bellavitis, Palazzo Guadagnini that has an elegant window with five lights in the central part of the façade, and the Casa Sale located just opposite. Also in the western part of the city, the map by dal Ponte shows the Palazzo Nardini and the Casa Bombardini-Baggio along Via Margnan, the Casa Priuli overlooking the river and the Contra' Pusterla (according to a common custom of other Venetian families, like the Belegno family and the Cappello family). Just beyond the Ponte Vecchio on Via Menarola are the Casa Beltrame and the Casa Nardini. While in the more central part of the village, to the buildings mentioned earlier we can add Palazzo Negri between the Terraglio and Via Gamba.

Several buildings are located along the axis of Via Nova (now Via Roma and continuing into Via Beata Giovanna) such as the Palazzo Balbi next to the Castello Inferiore, Casa Parolini at the end of the largest park in Bassano, and the Palazzo Remondini

▲ 74-76. At the top of the page is a view of the upper part of the façade of Palazzo Perli-Padovani: it appeared on the map by dal Ponte, but was dramatically transformed at the beginning of the 18th century. On the side the window with five lights that distinguishes the central part of the façade of Palazzo Guadagnini which combines both late gothic and Lombard elements. Both buildings rise along Via Verci, once called Campo Fiore. Below, between the two buildings that close Piazza Garibaldi on the east, you can see the massive Palazzo Negro from the second half of the 16th century distinguished by the high open galleries with its rusticated pillars. ▼

which is almost opposite to Santa Maria della Misericordia. Not far from the axis established by the Padovani we can see Palazzo Brocchi, initially owned by the merchants of Venetian silk. The western area of the city is poorer in such examples, although we must remember the Palazzo Negro at the crossing of Via Barbieri and Via dal Ponte. Continuing our journey along Via dal Ponte, we find the Palazzo Compostella.

Dating from between the Renaissance period and the 18th century revival, we find located on Via Marinali, the Palazzo del Tribunale (previously Antonibon) with two windows with three lights one over the other on a porch with a lowered arc. The most interesting buildings from the 18th century along the axis running from the river to Vialle delle Fosse, are Palazzo Sturm (previously Ferrari, now the center of the Museum of the Ceramics) and the Palazzo Bonfadini located at the southwest corner of Piazza della Libertà, Palazzo Roberti (now a bookshop, where it is possible to view on the noble floor the frescos by Giovanni Scajario, depicting stories of Anthony and Cleopatra). The Palazzo Scolari Marin, designed by Gaidon in 1770, next to the chapel of the Angel, and the large and irregular size of Palazzo Chiminelli along Viale dei Martiri are not any less interesting.

▲ *77-78. Above, a detail of the west wall of the salon on the piano nobile of Palazzo Roberti, depicting* The Stories of Anthony and Cleopatra *by Giovanni Scajario (1779). Below the salon of Palazzo Sturm rich in fresco and stucco decorations (1765-1766).* ▼

An Ideal Scenery for the Villas

The Bassano outskirts have naturally favored this type of architecture that usually shows in its most outstanding examples, the various and stratified interventions and the wise mixture of shapes and tastes that it is famous for.

«Next to this village the river Brenta flows and is plentiful with delicious fish. This place is famous for its precious wines that are made here, for the fruits that grow here, and much more for the courtesy of the master». With these words Andrea Palladio ended in his treaty of architecture (1570) the description of the Villa he said to have designed for his noble friend, the Conte Giacomo Angarano. The Conte stood in for Palladio at his daughter's wedding when he was away from Vicenza and the architect dedicated to him the first two books of his treaty.
The Villa, later acquired by the Gradenigo family and now owned by the Bianchi-Michiel family, can be considered thanks to its author, the most prestigious of those located along the river, on the foothills, or on the adjoining roads around the city of Bassano. The mild climate, the luxury and abundance of its natural scenery seem to favor this kind of settlement, so typical in the Venetian region.
Villa Bianchi-Michiel, a large, majestic three floored residence at Angarano can be approached by following Viale Scalabrini for a few kilometers. Its remarkable relief decorations have historical relevance amongst the Villas in the Bassano territory. The scholars have adequately demonstrated that Palladio realized the elegant *barchesse* (service buildings) with Tuscan columns that were located lateral to the site where the noble's quarters should have been located, and where Giacomo Angarano had a preexisting building. Over the course of the

▲ *79-80. The panoramic view of the façade of the villa planned by Andrea Palladio for the Count Giacomo Angaran (see below a sketch from the* Quattro Libri). *The building, today Bianchi-Michiel, underwent many successive dramatic transformations.* ▼

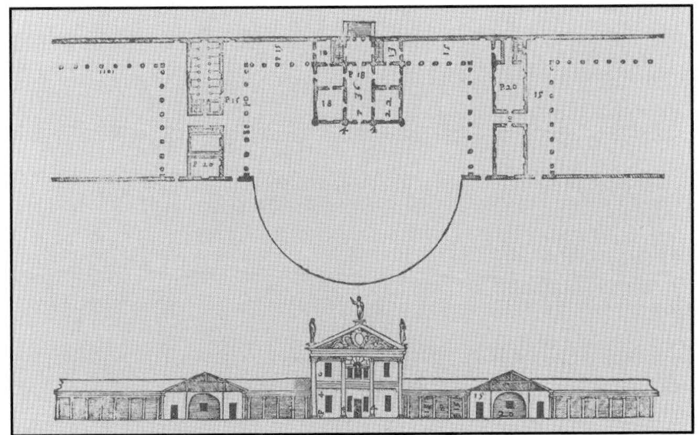

18th century Domenico Margutti's design changed radically its dimensions and style.
Such continuous interventions on previous buildings, nearly never coming to a definitive outcome, seem to sum up the erratic styles of the architecture of Bassano's villas. This is what happened with another complex, set up by the Angarano family, the so-called Villa San Giuseppe, now the property of the Jesuits. The late 16th century part, with rusticated walls around the ground floor, with Doric and Ionic orders correctly placed one over the other, and the elegance of the vaults of the porch was designed by an anonymous planner who could not avoid the influence of the Palladian era. The same was true in the very elongated façade of Ca' Erizzo located north of the city in the area of Margnan, at La Nave (where the ferry used to stop) along the bank of the river. The numerous owners that followed, from the 16th century to today, made modifications, additions, extensions, and re-

▲ *81-83. Sides view of the 16th century façade of Ca' Erizzo at Margnan, where the first nucleus of expansion of Bassano began. Below a view of the villa designed by an anonymous architect for the powerful family dei Priuli towards the middle of the 17th century. Below on the left the fresco of Palazzo Bonaguro at Angarano, a building which could considered both a city residence and a Villa.* ◀ ▼

storations (especially in the course of the 17th century, when the interior frescos were painted; but the external had been decorated two centuries earlier by Jacopo dal Ponte).

Two other Villas at Angarano testify to greater homogeneity. They can be reached by continuing beyond Casa Bianchi-Michiel along the Strada dei Pilati. The first is the Villa Brocchi-Colonna which conserves the original inner aspect. Into its façade two interesting Logge were built one above the other. The second is the Villa Roberti from the 18th century at San Giorgio. Although only the left portion was completed, the asymmetry does not compromise the evocative rigor of the façade which gives the impression of it leaning against the hill you can see in the background.

Two other buildings have lost their original country look since they are now incorporated into the dense development of Angarano, just beyond the Ponte Vecchio. They are Palazzo Bonaguro, a massive and imposing 16th century structure later refurnished with a wide rear garden located on Via Angarano, and the Villa Priuli in the elegant taste of Longhena.

▲ *84-86. Villa di Ca' Rezzonico certainly is, together with villa Bianchi-Michiel, the most impressive suburban building. The Villa was first commissioned in the 18th century by the powerful Venetian family, which was protected by their relative Pope Clemente XIII, and built in different phases involving the work of very important artists such as Massari, Abbondio Stazio, Volpato, Canova, Pellegrini, and Gaidon. Although it can be considered quite consistent, the complex is an effective synthesis of the many architectural styles of suburban Bassano. In this example, the 18th century rapports between the sections of the building are incorporated into the early 16th century style of the villa-castle (see for example the four corner towers), and the intricate delicacy and opulence of the interior decorations with the raw power of the exterior aspect. Here below a view of the 19th century Parolini Garden founded in 1805 by Alberto from Bassano, the first example in Veneto of an authentic botanical garden excluding the university orchards. It features plants from India, China, Mexico, and California. Amongst the different species there is also a* pinus Parolinia, *a variety discovered in Greece on Mount Ida.* ▼

Remondini City: a Paper World

In the 18th century a company employed one inhabitant out of eight, the printing office Remondini. It took all over the world its sensibility for images, curiosity for natural science and culture, and passion for the arts. A mixture of Hollywood, Disneyland and Detroit.

Between the 17th and 18th centuries Bassano became one of the most important industrial centers of the Veneto State. The Remondini Printing office was a company that surpassed all others. The relationship between Bassano and the Remondini as it is described in the *Encyclopedia* by Diderot and Alembert, could be compared to that between the cities of Turin and Fiat, Detroit and General Motors, and Eindhoven and Philips. It had 18 typographical presses, 30 chalcographic ones, four paper mills (so they could autonomously supply the raw materials), an appropriate foundry for the creation of typographical characters, and more then one thousand employees in a city of 8,000 inhabitants. It had as many sales agents, the Tesini, that covered the entire world on foot reaching Saint Petersburg, Latin America, London, and Paris, while the company was engaged to support their families, as some sort of advanced payment. Furthermore it had astonishing sales for correspondence, with its catalogue that was proudly modernized every few years and the company paying the shipment expenses. The Remondini Printing office was one of the main productive colossusses of preindustrial Europe. It was a privately-owned company, not supported by the privilege of the court (thus not entrusting itself to the possibility of political prices) and deeply rooted in the very center of the city (on the northern margin of the Piazza San Giovanni, now Piazza della Libertà). It was founded in the second half of the 17th century by Giovanni Antonio Remondini and was in con-

87-89. Above the Remondini houses facing the northern side of Piazza Libertà: here was the headquarters of the large 18th century editorial company. Below on the left, a decorated paper from the first half of the 19th century with ornamental landscapes of Bassano amongst which the famous bridge. On the right a popular religious print depicting Saint Rocco (18th century).

90. Ritratto di Bartolomeo ▸ Gamba *(Portrait of Bartolomeo Gamba) 1816, by Francesco Roberti (1789-1857), located in the Museum of Bassano. Gamba was for many years the director of the Remondini printing shop. He was a passionate lover of books, and later, after the acquisition of the typography of Alvisopoli, he became the most important editor of his time in Veneto.*

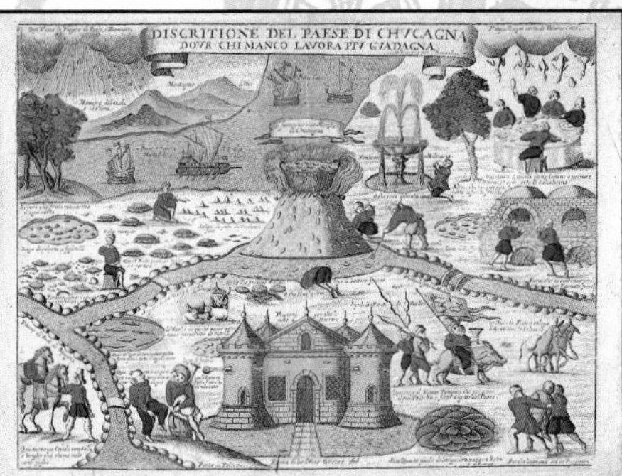

▴ *91-93. Two of the best known prints by Remondini are (above)* Il Paese di Cuccagna *(The land of plenty), from the end of the 18th century, and (below)* Il Cane Barbino *also from the 18th century. On the background of this page another success of the Remondini printing shop, the famous* Gioco dell'oca *(The Goose Game).* ▾

stant development in the following century, until the unavoidable nineteenth-century crisis. An exemplary independent business model, which produced trees, cellulose, paper, and press characters. It also included a prestigious school specializing in engraving (where some of the greatest specialists like the brothers Dal Pedro, Cristoforo Dall'Aqua, and the great Giovanni Volpato came from). The company was encouraged constantly by the Veneto State in competition with the traditional powers of the field (Augsburg, Paris, London), so to limit the amount of expensive import products from foreign countries. The capillary distribution network concurred to photograph in real time the changing tastes of the public. Remondini therefore had a very high demand in the market of popular prints, and was winning competitive wars while not always respecting what today we would recognize as copyright. At the same time they asserted themselves in the field of valuable engravings, thanks to the systematic acquisitions of sheets and antique copper engraved by renown craftsmen from the 16th and 17th centuries, most of which were left in inheritance in the course of the 1800's to the collections of the city Museum. Bassano in the Remondini era becomes the "paper city", open to the influence of cultures from every corner of the world. It provided wallpaper, lining for furniture and an inexhaustible source of other objects for the industry of education and for entertainment (playing cards, maps of the world, atlases, business cards, etc. and the optical views, an anticipation of the motion pictures).

The Fragile Beauty of Images

In the 16th and 17th centuries Bassano and its surroundings, in particular Nove, become one of the European capitals of ceramics and china, and produced an impressive number of objects for daily life.

The arc comprised between the 1600's and the 1700's (in particular the 17th century) begins the great era of Bassano ceramics. The Antonibon Manufactures in the nearby village of Nove was one of the greatest and more qualified companies of the time in this field. Some environmental conditions favored their success. The neighboring hills (from Marostica to Romano) guaranteed deposits of clay and white earth which was indispensable for its work. The Brenta supplied sufficient hydraulic energy to the mills for the crushing of the quartz and carbonate of calcium («molini pestasassi») in order to stir the pastes. It was also a comfortable route in which to trade them. The strategic position of the city ultimately favored the spread of their products.
Also in this case the productive activity was registered in the center of the city. The most important in all of the Serenissima was the case of the Manardi manufactures from 1669 to 1719. For a long period of time it was believed to be located in the village of Angarano, therefore outside of the town-walls, but it was instead located, as recent discoveries have proved, inside the city walls, at the crossing of Via Campo Marzio and Via Portici Lunghi. It is here that traces have been found (that soon will become visitable) of an ancient furnace for the settling of the clay. Amongst the most celebrated products by Manardi were the so-called *latesini*, majolica works of great levity, which derived their name from the *latteo*, enamel with which they came covered in.

▲ *94-96. Next to the title, the* Artigiano *(The Craftsman) 1984 by Federico Bonaldi. Above from the Museum of Bassano, a large wall panel normally placed under a window, made in majolica by the Antonibon manufacturers in Nove (1751). Below the Manardi houses which were the headquarters of the most important manufacturers of ceramics and majolica in Bassano in the 17th century.* ▼

97-104. From the top clockwork wise: a light blue enamel majolica plate with blue polychromatic decorations; a porcelain consommé bowl with a polychromatic landscape decoration; Alessio Tasca, Rozzampia *(1979), extrusion, grès, enamels with ash; Pompeo Pianezzola,* Open Book *(1998), red refractory, reagent, and enamel; a soup-tureen in majolica with polychromatic decorations; a china plate with polychromatic decorations of a Venetian scene; a china plate with polychromatic decoration; a porcelain consommé bowl very finely decorated with polychrome in a floral design.*

Another important factory, the Moretti-Marinoni, was situated in the vicinity of the city, in Rivarotta, at the extreme southern edge of the village of Angarano (traditionally a recognized center of similar factories), near the border of Nove. Here Alessio Tasca has restored in over ten years of passionate work an «ancient factory of glaze and red earth», most likely with a 16th century foundation.

The 18th century is referred to because of the extraordinary spread of objects in ceramics (not only pottery for the kitchen, but also tables, frames, and wall lights). Compared to the "world of paper" that Remondini operated in Bassano, this field saw prevail in that phase the manufactures in Nove, against European contenders (the factory of china in Meissen founded in 1710 by Augusto il Forte di Sassonia).

In reality we find ourselves facing the other side of the coin which is the desire to fill up our daily lives with shapes and images and with the creations of artists and craftsmen.

It is not by chance if many images found on the decorations of objects in ceramics derive with striking similarity from prints and etchings from the Remondini.

After the 19th century crisis the productions were of less quality (white earth "wares"), but in the last few decades the ceramics department in the area of Bassano has seen rejuvenation, returning to assert itself. Today there are over 400 workshops with more than 2,600 employees.

THE ORIGIN OF MODERN BASSANO

THE 19TH CENTURY DOES NOT DETERMINE NEW EXTENSIONS APART FROM THE CLAIMING OF SOME RELIGIOUS STRUCTURES FOR CIVIL FUNCTIONS. BASSANO DOES NOT GROW, BUT WITH THE DESTRUCTION OF ANCIENT THE WALLS, ITS IMAGE BECOMES ALTERED AND IT IS UP TO PAINTING TO RECOVER IT.

The fall of the Serenissima (1797) starts in Bassano a rather long phase of economic stagnation, with marginal modifications of the city plan and of the shape of the city. The communal census proves that not even one new house was built between 1816 and 1866, even if numerous buildings were restored and restructured.
The Napoleonic abolition of many religious complexes had rendered available for public functions (schools, hospitals, rest and shelter houses) some important and central buildings. In 1831 the hospital was transferred from the monastery of San Francesco to the cenoby of the Reformati. This was followed a few years later (in 1840) by the Franciscan monastery that accommodated the Museum of the city, a reading room (later a library) and the gymnasium.
The only intervention *ex-novo* of some relevance turns out to be the neoclassic Social Theatre in Contra' delle Grazie (today Viale dei Martiri) by Giacomo Bauto in 1805, in which the extreme interventions by the architect Gaidon can be found.
The economic crisis cannot however cancel the longing for modernity although sometimes progress implies conflicting choices. The new communal cemetery of 1822 near Santa Croce represents an important example. Examples of urban *maquillage* can be seen in the statue of Giuseppe Garibaldi in the public square dedicated to him in 1883, the erection of the obelisk in honor of Vittorio Emanuele II also in 1883, and the construction of a small Piazza with a monument dedicated to Jacopo

▲ *105-106. Above, a foreshortening view of the Teatro Sociale, designed by Giacomo Bauto in 1805, along the viale dei Martiri, which you can observe in the view below.* ▼

dal Ponte. Unfortunately there were many episodes of destruction.

The demolition of the northern and eastern portions of the curtain of the wall, started in 1886, was the cause of much controversy. The demolition of the walls near Porta delle Grazie supplied the city with a spectacular view of the mouth of the Valsugana, while the one along the side on the Fosse satisfied the new needs of modern traffic. This definitively cancelled the ancient image of the city. The railway station in 1877 had been placed west, consequently marking this entire sector of the city with connecting arteries, roads and railways.

It does not astonish us that one of the main features of 19th century painting in Bassano, surely in agreement with what was happening in the rest of Italy, but also reflecting specific variations such as seen in the works of Roberto Roberti or Antonio Marinoni, Gaspare Fontana and Federico Moja, becomes a nostalgic desire to follow the thread of history in the signs of the past reduced to ruins, to return to the ancient shape of the free borough and its frescoed buildings.

▲ *107-109. Above in a photograph from 1878, the demolition of a section of the 13th century wall. Here to the side, a foreshortening of Piazzetta Jacopo dal Ponte, one of the few significant interventions of the 19th century of an urban vessel. Below, Antonio Marinoni's (Bassano 1796-1871),* Veduta di Bassano from San Vito towards Margnan and Angarano *(1840-1841).* ▶ ▼

The City Outside the Walls

In the 20th century the ancient Bassano becomes the historical center of the city, comprising mainly of shops and offices. The city is expanded at first south, then more decidedly to the east, modifying the designation of these areas.

The history of the city Bassano in the past century is characterized, as it happened in many other Italian cities and abroad, by the impressive expansion beyond the ancient limits of what today is called the "historical center" of a much wider urban center.
The key date in this transformation is 1907 when a new bridge was planned to be built beside the wooden one, so to relieve the increasing traffic of the city. At the same time a start was made on a new cathedral, which would replace outside the walls, the ancient Pieve di Santa Maria in Colle. The building, after the terrible vicissitudes of the First World War, was classified as an ossuarium for the thousands of fallen. It was only inaugurated in 1936.
The axis defined by the Ponte Nuovo and the ossarium, opposite the walls of the Bastion, not only gives the outer ring roads a completed outline, but also determines the estimated direction of urban expansion, almost repeating with a different inclination, the axis of the 14th century Via Nova. In effect since the start of the century, the first working class quarter had been established between the bridge and the Ossarium, not far from Via Bonaguro.
These criteria for urban development tended to specialize in the city quarters although a wider expansion occurs in the eastern direction. The residential areas that were more prestigious were concentrated in the area beyond Viale Fosse and close to the new Viale Venezia developing a quarter of detached houses. While the quarters in the south and south-east, following the rise of the mighty

110-112. Here above, an inspection of the Ponte Nuovo, in a photo from 1917. Below are two examples of the transformation of the buildings, for commercial purposes, in the historical center.

enamel industry in 1924, lodged the houses for the working class who had gradually abandoned the historic center. This caused heavy deterioration and damage, a situation that has been dealt with in the last decades with visible success.

The town planning inside the old circle of walls also started to change considerably. The demand for new shops on the ground floor of several buildings inevitably ravaged the original façade of many buildings. This continued until a series of protection norms for the preservation of historical buildings were approved in 1924 and concurred to slacken the disfiguring phenomenon. But the prevailing destination of the city center for both commercial and public functions continued to grow without seeming to slow down.

In spite of the problems that almost all the historical centers have met in the last century, in spite of persistent issues of traffic with daily blocks connecting arteries and fast routes, Bassano has managed to preserve its charm as a small capital city at the foot of the PreAlps. Its geographic location, still strategic, garantees such natural beauties to justify a millennial choice.

113-116. In the three pictures above some examples of Liberty architecture in the residential area which develops from the axis of viale Venezia. Below a view of the working class housing in the quarter of Bonaguro built from 1905 from the project by the engineer Indri.

Bassano and the First World War

In the front line, at the foot of one of the mountains in which it was fought most fiercly, the city, that only after the war took the name of Bassano del Grappa, was totally evacuated in the winter of 1917. The monuments within the city.

In the course of the First World War (1915-1918), and especially after the Italian defeat at Caporetto (October 24, 1917), the city of Bassano found itself in the front line. In the previous months it had faced a series of economic crises due partly to the thousands of Italalian emigrants coming back from other European countries at war. From that moment on it became a temporary shelter for the fleeing soldiers and for the thousands of civilians threatened by the Austro-Hungarian troops. In a few days as the enemies artillery approached, the city had to be totally evacuated leaving only 200 people behind in order to prevent looting while impressive caravans hastily transported the rest of the population (14,000 people) along the road to Rosà and Padova.

The damages to the historical center were only marginal (250 buildings were destroyed or at least damaged), thanks to the resistance of the front-line on Monte Grappa. The Ponte Vecchio, previously bombed in September of 1915, escaped destruction and for the soldiers who observed it from the trenches, became a symbol of the Native land that resisted (after the Nazis in retreat had mined it, it was the Alpines themselves who did their utmost for its reconstruction). However the war left its mark on the city plan: not only with the monument from 1938 overlooking the Valsugana at the end of the Viale delle Fosse and dedicated to the commander of the Fourth Army, General Gaetano Giardino (also recalled in so many names of roads

▲ *117-118. Above, the monument erected in 1938 to commemorate the General Gaetano Giardino, in viale delle Fosse, which we can observe below, and some tracked cannons parked along the viale in 1916.* ▼

and places). The new cathedral, which had been restored in the first decade of the century, became an Ossarium conserving the remains of approximately 6,000 soldiers. The imposing neo-gothic construction, in red brick, with a double bell tower and the façade decorated with pinnacles, dominates Piazzale Cadorna, recently embellished by a great fountain by the sculptor Natalino Andolfatto from Pove.

Because of the conflict which had made Mount Grappa a crucial place of courageous defense and the stage of the victorious conclusion of the war («Mount Grappa you are my homeland», sings one of the most famous war songs of our recent history), the city changed its name, assuming in 1928, that of Bassano del Grappa.

▲ *119-122. Above and on the lower margin to the right, the Tempio Ossario. It was initially built to substitute the old Cathedral (in the forefront the large fountain by Natalino Andolfatto). Here below is an example of the destruction that the city suffered during the war.* ▼

Mount Grappa

The mountain *par excellance* of the city for centuries supplied stone, lumber, pastures and cheese. A center of alpine excursions since the end of the 19th century, it was a theatre of terrible military operations during the 1st World War and of the partisan struggle against Nazi-fascism.

The Grappa is a calcareous massif comprised on a perimeter of approximately 100 km, between the Brenta and Piave rivers, to the northeast of the city of Bassano. The maximum height, to the top, about 31.5 km from the city, is of 1,775 metres. Geologically interested by karst phenomena, the mountain lacks superficial waters. This has not prevented the growth of flora of great importance characterized by 37 various species of elegant spontaneous orchids. The quaternary glaciation have only marginally touched the area, so that it has been transformed into a shelter for different species of vegetation of the Tertiary Period. The steepest slope is the most southern. Its name means "tip", summit, and hook. For many thousand years it has been a natural resource of firewood and for construction, its woods and forests were fought over by the communities of the area and it offered stone quarries which are now abandoned, and pastures for the herds. Towards the end of the 19th century it has become an unavoidable destination for the first experiences of hiking. The Italian Alpine Club promoted in 1897 the construction of a shelter near the summit.

It was only during the First World War that the massif was equipped with roads, while up to that moment the connections especially for the transport of goods were assured by a thick net of mule-tracks. The main road of access, just beyond Romano d'Ezzelino, is still today the Strada Cadorna, constructed between 1916 and 1917 by General Francesco, so that it was protected from the fire

▲ *123-125. Next to the title is a view of the memorial chapel on Mount Grappa. Here above* Veduta del Grappa verso i Colli Alti *(1850-1853). Below in the forefront is a photo of protected wild flowers on Mount Grappa.* ▼

▲ *126-127. A footpath on Mount Grappa. Below the* Via Eroica *(The Road of Heroes), which is marked by 14 memorial stones that show where the harshest battle of the war was fought. It leads to the* Portale di Roma *by Alessandro Limongelli, and to the War Museum. From here it climbs up to the observatory terrace that offers an extraordinary view of the valley.* ▼

of artilleries that came from north. Another imposing war construction is the gallery Vittorio Emanuele III that you can partially visit, and penetrates for nearly a kilometer and a half under the summit. With secondary detours, it develops for over 5 kilometers. Here were situated the Italian artilleries with 23 batteries of cannons which prevented the breakthrough of the front by the Austro-Hungarian troops, after the defeat of Caporetto. After the military actions in November-December 1917, two more battles were fought on the slopes of the mountains. The first was on June 1918 and the second one in the last days of the conflict, in the second half of October (this one caused the deaths of more than 5,000 men).

The entire area over 1,700 m. has been declared a national monument and a sacred zone. The top esplanade accommodates the majestic Sacrario of the Italian dead (12,615 of which 10,322 unknown), completely realized in stone from Mount Grappa by Giovanni Greppi and Giannino Castiglioni. Inaugurated in 1935 it rises on a structure surmounted by the grave of General Giardino and by the chapel of the Madonnina which was initially consecrated in 1901 to be auspicious for the new century by the patriarch of Venice Giuseppe Sarto, the future Pope Pio X and later to become a saint. It was later transformed into a sanctuary in 1921. On the northern ridge of the Italian Sacrarium the Austro-Hungarian Ossario was built for more than 10,000 of their dead, nearly all without a name.

A Gold Medal

It was assigned to the city in order to celebrate its heroic behavior during the terrible biennium of 1944-45. It is a history page that reaffirms the relationship between Bassano and Mount Grappa.

On the 9th of October 1946, the Prime Minister of the newly constituted Italian Republic, Alcide De Gasperi, awarded to Bassano del Grappa a gold medal for military valor, and for the behavior held by its citizens during the war of liberation from the Nazi-Fascism (September 1943 to April 1945).
Between the rivers Brenta and Piave the statement of reasons reads from the memorial slab (on the side wall of the church of San Francesco that overlooks the Piazza Garibaldi) that for 20 months of war occupation Volunteers for Freedom fought in epic deeds of war against the invading enemy. This noble city along with the territory of the Grappa sacrificed on the passes 171 young lives and 682 of its children in front of the firing squads. It bore the martyrdom of the 804 convicts, the 3,270 prisoners, and the destruction of 700 burnt down houses.
In the impossibility to give back the conflicting feelings of those years, the fear and the courage, the ferocity and the destruction, this remains an emblematic and pitiless accounting of a civil war. As a result the town and the mountain were tied again in a bond which became possibly stronger than the one established in the First World War. It was here that the partisans formations who formed in the first months of 1944 ("Italy Free-Archeson", "Italy Free-Field Cross", "Matteotti", "Garibaldi", in two detachments) had gathered and operated. And it was on the slopes of the mountain that the most terrible episode

128-129. Above is a view of Via Santa Maria delle Grazie where on September 26, 1944, 31 partisans were hung. After the liberation the name of the road was changed to Viale dei Martiri. Below along the same road the entrance of the partisans in Bassano at the end of the war.

▲ 130-132. *Above a picture of the Ponte Nuovo after the aerial bombing by the allies. On the right side the entrance to the Tempio Ossario which was devastated by the bombing. Below, American tanks parade from the Piazza Libertà to Piazza Garibaldi on April 30, 1945.* ▼ ▶

of circumstance took place (the mopping-up of Mount Grappa September 20-23, 1944).

About one thousand partisans faced up to a Nazi-fascist contingent (SS, Black Brigades, battalions of the RSI, Ukrainian units and Alpenjäger units) that were ten times more numerous and much better equipped. It was a severe massacre with about 500 dying. Less than one third of the partisans units survived the systematic annihilation that, with the destruction of all the mountain barns, had prevented for long months the resumption of activity on the part of the Resistance. The mopping-up was sealed by two pitiless mass executions. The first was on the 24th of September when 14 young people were forced to dig their grave and then were sentenced to the firing squad, and the second came two days later when 31 others were hung by the neck with their corpses left to hang for days in the trees along the way of Santa Maria delle Grazie, hence the name of Viale dei Martiri (of the martyrs).

The first partisan struggle was resumed only at the end of the winter of 1945 by the survivors who re-united in the "Martyrs of the Mount Grappa Brigade". On the 16th of February the Ponte Vecchio which was the last passage across the river Brenta was shined in order to avert the allied bombings that would have been more destructive. Because Bassano was bombed, as we have read in the statement for the gold medal, this contributed to the modifying for the last time in any substantial terms, the historical city center.

THE GRAPPA

TERMINATIONE
Degl'Illustrissimi, & Eccellentiss. Signori
DEPVTATI ALLA CAMERA
DEL COMERCIO.
De dì 30. Luglio 1722.
In essecutione di Decreto dell' Eccellentissimo Senato 11. Genaro 1719.
In Materia dell'Arti di questa Dominante, che riguarda l'Arte dell'Acqua Vita.

Stampata per Z. Antonio, & Almorò Pinelli, Stampatori Ducali.

A BY-PRODUCT, POMACE IS THE RESULT OF DISTILLATION PERFECTED THROUGH THE CENTURIES. FROM RURAL CULTURE, BETWEEN LAND AND SOUL, A WIDE ESTABLISHED PRODUCT IN ITALY AND ALL OVER THE WORLD. IN BASSANO A MUSEUM CELEBRATES ITS FAME.

The history of distillation is ancient, dating back to Egyptian times, and is usually associated with the highest ranks of society and practices mixing philosophy and magic such as alchemy which sought the elixir of life. The Middle Ages greeted the production of an alcoholic liquid, called *aqua ardens* (hot water) as it was inflammable but the use of *aqua vitis* (translating the Arabic term for alcohol *al-kohol*, literally "the rarefied thing") perfected in Modern times, thanks also to Michele Savonarola, a doctor from Padova. It was regarded as a pharmacological remedy for epidemics and the plague, as one of the two possible meanings of its name (water from the vine or water of life) generated significant confusion.

Although the history of grappa is quite different, it is not less interesting. It is firmly fastened to a material and peasant culture. The origin of the word is probably from the Medieval Latin term "grappulus" clearly explaining that grappa comes from the pomace, which is the solid part of grapes consisting of skin and grape seeds discarded in the processing of wine. Up to the 19th century, discards were used in the production of *vinello*, where the water was barely colored with often putrid pomace and destined for the consumption of the lower classes.

Therefore grappa is the only *acquavite* extracted from a poor solid matter (cognac, for example comes from the distillation of a wine from a specific area in France). For centuries it was limited to a rough rural production, which explains the lack of

written evidence about its origin. This strengthening liqueur has become through the refining of the distillation process and instruments, more of a habit in the city life on an international scale. It embodies that special aptitude that knows how to capture the pleasures of life from discarded products.
The history of *grappa*, illustrated by the techniques and machinery which for the last century have made possible the production of this quality liqueur (basically intermittent cycle stills with direct fire or steam boilers which sets the difference between the high quality artisan product and the less esteemed industrial *grappa*) is permanently on show in the center of Bassano both in the old tavern of Bortolo Nardini on the Ponte Vecchio and in the Museum of Grappa which was opened by the Distillerie Poli in the 16th century Case Beltrame, in Via Gamba.

133-138. Next to the title, the Edict of the Serenissima regarding the guild of the grappa makers, founded in 1601. To the left, the intermittent cycle still with direct fire boiler in the Poli Museum. Above on the left the entrance to the Museum of Grappa, and on the right is a still with an air cooling cone which belonged to the Dutch doctor Ermanno Boerhaave (1668-1738). Below the interior of the famous Grapperia Nardini on the Ponte Vecchio. At the bottom of the text is an etching of a still from Commentarii Pedacii Dioscoridis Anazarbei de Materia Madica, *Venezia 1565.*

The First Museum on Terraferma

Founded in 1840, the Museum of Bassano is also a library and an archive. It reflects every multicolored and precious treasure of the city.

A small painting by Antonio Viviani depicts the early aspect of the Museum on the opening day in 1840 in the convent of San Francesco, the first example of a public collection in the mainland towns. Since then, the Museum has been constantly growing, enriched by many donations and bequests, which continue to this day. It still has an exceptional variety in the same building of handmade items, paintings, books, and documents. Its unusual diversity makes the Museum the perfect reflection of Bassano's millennial culture.

The main section of the Museum is the Franciscan monastery facing Piazza Garibaldi, but equally important are Palazzo Strum along Via Ferracina, overlooking the river Brenta, which features ceramic and natural science collections, as well as the temporary exhibitions in Palazzo Agostinelli along Via Barbieri, and Palazzo Bonaguro along Via Angarano near the Ponte Vecchio. In the third decade of the 19th century, the bequest of Giambattista Brocchi improves the public collection of the city. The naturalist bequeaths not only the scientific finds collected over many years of explorations in Italy and abroad, but also included a considerable library, which was later enlarged during the 19th century. As it happens the substantial library integrated the painting collection, whose provenance were public buildings, such as the Palazzo Pretoria's Natural Science Gallery, and religious institutions that had closed down and had been subsequently demolished. After the public hospital had

▲ *139-141. Above, the* Inaugurazione del Museo Civico di Bassano *(1848) by Antonio Viviani (1797-1854) conserved in the Museum of Bassano. Below, two views of the cloister of San Francesco hosting the Museum of inscribed plaques and tablets, and access to the main Museum.* ▼

▲ *142-144. Above, another view of the cloister of San Francesco. Below, the lower arch from where the stairs that lead to the Pinacoteca start, and a view of the central room dedicated to 17th and 18th century paintings.* ▼

been moved from San Francesco to the monastery of the Riformati, on the opposite side of Viale delle Fosse, the Franciscan complex was destined to hold the most varied collections of cultural interest, as the Library Archive Museum of Bassano still does until these days. Amongst the 19th century donations, the one of Giambattista Remondini, acquired in 1849, boasts of a priceless studio of drawings and printed works, the core of the homonymous printing shop, including numerous engravings by Dürer. A few years later the Canovian fund was acquired, donated by Giambattista Sartori Canova, the great sculptor's step-brother, which included sketches, temperas, plaster casts, about 2,000 drawings, a collection of letters, and the library.

At the moment the artistic wealth of this world renown Museum consists of 500 paintings, 20,000 prints, 4,000 drawings, sculptures, coin collections, natural science, and so much else that an extension to the vast building of the Museum seems to be needed.

The 17th century cloister, which welcomes the visitor, hosts the collection of inscribed and carved stones. On the ground floor to the left there are protohistoric and archaeological collections, the Apulian ceramics donated by Professor Virgilio Chini, and to the right are the library and the drawing and print studio.

On the first floor, starting from the central octagonal hall, in the three main wings recently decorated, there are to the left the largest public collection of paintings by Jacopo dal Ponte, to the right the exceptional Canovian fund (an extensive visit should be paid to the gallery of plaster casts at Possagno, Antonio Canova's birth town, not far from Bassano) and to the center the 17th and 18th century paintings. Other sections exhibit medieval art, 19th and 20th century collections and the small size paintings from the 15th and 16th centuries. The two main funds owned by the city Museum, are the Canovian and the dal Ponte funds. They contribute to the international interest revolving around it which regularly hosts, in the Chilesotti Room on the ground floor, lectures and conferences of international interest. The 18th century Palazzo Sturm, donated to the city in 1942 by Baron Sturm Von Hirschfield, hosts on a permanent exhibition, an outstanding ceramic collection with several hundred pieces from between the 14th and the 20th centuries. It witnesses a fundamental aspect of the local culture within the sphere of minor arts. The edifice is specially suited to the task and was built shortly after 1750 and was frescoed by Giorgio Anselmi. With the

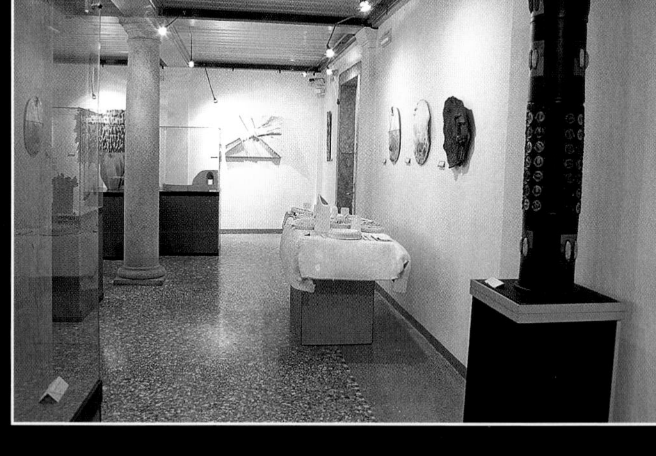

paintings by Gaetano Zompini in the chamber and also decorated with an elegant stucco, the palace reflects for the period and taste, the most significant part of the public collections of Bassano. Anyone sightseeing in Bassano absolutely cannot deprive themselves of a visit to the complex of the museums of the city, the precious, accurate, and lovingly guarded heart of its memories.

▲ 145-148. Above a charming picture of the exterior of Palazzo Sturm, where the Museum of Ceramics is located (the left page shows two views of the exhibits). Below, a view of the wing dedicated to the great artist Antonio Canova in the city Museum where on exhibition is the very important bequest to the city from the artist's step-brother, monsignor Gianbattista Sartori Canova. ▼

Cittadella Marostica Possagno
Esagono
Veneto delle Grazie
Castelfranco Bassano Asolo

The Culture of Food

Fragrances and tastes refer to the beautiful nature and a widespread love for the culinary arts which make Bassano an inviting reference point for connoisseurs of great food.

White asparagus, sprouting broccoli, wild herbs, mushrooms, and radicchio are only some of the key ingredients in Bassano's gastronomy. Some of these are exclusive products to the area, such as the delicious and famous white asparagus, and have had an important role in many culinary pages in the local gastronomy texts, thanks to the inventive talents of the local chefs widely known as ambassadors of this area. Their experience, professionalism, and their ability of marrying tradition to novelty, have started a gastronomical project mixing both touristic and cultural aspects.

This sector moves around a world of historical research, scientific studies, culinary experimentation, competence, friendliness, and hospitality. In every season the fertile land of Bassano offers unique produce that inspires the chef's imagination when revising recipes, recovering old ones, and creating new ones. Springtime is the best time of the year for wild herbs whose delicate and versatile tastes enhance all courses from *hors d'oeuvre* to desserts.

Springtime also brings triumph to the tables in Bassano with the arrival of its prince: the white asparagus, which connoisseurs have associated with Vespaiolo, a white wine produced in the nearby area of Breganze: unquestionable stars of an eno-gastronomic cycle of shows which take place between April and May, and cannot be missed.

Another typical produce, the *biso* (green pea) is cultivated along the strip of land at the foot of Mount Grappa and is also a main feature in the

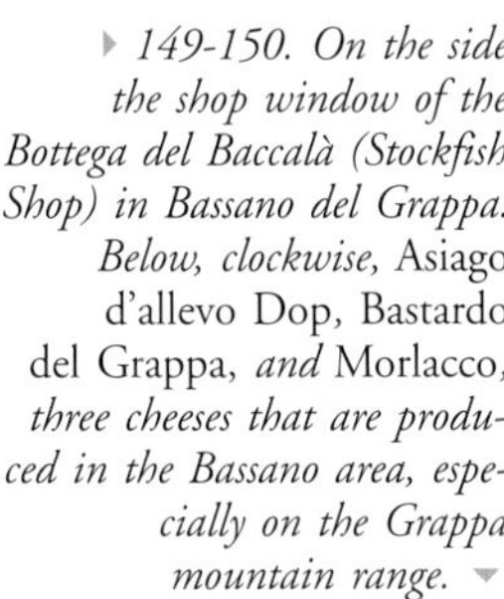

149-150. On the side the shop window of the Bottega del Baccalà (Stockfish Shop) in Bassano del Grappa. Below, clockwise, Asiago d'allevo Dop, Bastardo del Grappa, *and* Morlacco, *three cheeses that are produced in the Bassano area, especially on the Grappa mountain range.*

▸ *151-152. On the side a bunch of* Vespaiola *grapes which are widespread in the area of Bassano. Below, the typical Bassano dish: eggs and white asparagus.* ▾

culinary fair in June. As it happens also with the asparagus, this less known legumen is accompanied by Verdiso, a wine which enhances its taste and is obtained by an autochthonous vine from the Venetian foothill.

Ever-present on the table of this wonderful little city along the river Brenta are the finferli, chiodini, brise, and boletus mushrooms which are found both in the summer and autumn seasons.

Autumn brings back the meaty flavours typical of the region of Veneto such as horse, pork, wild boar, rabbit, guinea fowl, duck, poultry, quail, lamb, and goose. These are the variety of meats that are featured in "Autunno sull'aia" (Autumn in the Farm Yard), another successful fair operated by the restaurant owners. It is a wonderful opportunity to discover the traditional cuisine of the area.

The local cuisine not only features local produce but, in an area geographically far from the sea, restaurant owners have managed to stage "Pesce e Pittura in Quaresima" (Fish and Painting at Lent), a fair including both salt water and fresh water fish which is creatively prepared by the chefs of the numerous restaurants. Every night the fair exhibits a local artist who attends the reception and illustrates his or her work. And we must not forget the restaurants in the area of Bassano specializing in the preparation of the famous "Baccalà alla vicentina" (stockfish in Vicenza style), a much sought after and true delicacy. *(o.f.)*

Cities On Stage

One of the most important summer events in Veneto. Over 400 shows are held from July to August in the theaters of Bassano, and in the castles and villas, in the parks and squares of the towns in the foothill. A chance to discover the vast and fascinating cultural heritage of Veneto.

The Operaestate Festival Veneto was first started in 1981 simply as a summer opera event. Over the years the additions of theater, ballet, modern dance, music, and cinema programs have turned it into one of the most prestigious and popular summer events. This long fair has become of great importance over the last few years in both national reviews and in the Veneto area, where it has become second in the list of major events, offering two summer months full of quality performances and entertainment. The success of this event, due to its richness and variety, grows with every year, reaching a peak of almost 130,000 spectators.
Another peculiarity of the Bassano Festival is that it stretches far beyond the city of Bassano. Over the past few years, thanks to the support of the Veneto Region, numerous cities in the area have eagerly participated in the project adding to the title a new subheading, *Le città palcoscenico* (The Stage Cities). These cities and towns are places of architectural, historic, and landscape relevance in the Veneto area, and are transformed especially for the Bassano Festival into unusual but effective and beautiful stages. Villas, parks, and castles have evolved into true and permanent theater sets over the years, while Bassano, which hosts the operative offices for the event, offers several perfectly equipped open spaces. The largest is what used to be the Cimberle Ferrari barracks, now converted into a huge amphitheater which is an ideal stage for the most spectacular performances such as the best international dance, the most

▲ *153-154. The open air Cimberle Ferrari Theater, features over one thousand seats in an amphitheater, and a large stage, ideal for major events. Below, the Ezzelini Castle: the entrance to the area used as a theatre, the Ortazzo courtyard, runs along a scenic route along the torch lit walls.* ▼

important symphonic and jazz concerts, and great cinema. Amongst the historical buildings hosting live shows, the Castle of Ezzelini is probably the most charming of all. It is devoted to contemporary dance and theater, and live concerts by the best international jazz artists who join the annual music workshop in Bassano. The Parolini Gardens, the important botanical gardens in the center of the city, host an open air theater featuring an art film festival and the "Mini Fest", theatre shows for the children. Some sections of the festival take place in the Cloister of the city Museum which is most suited for quiet and thoughtful concerts and shows. But the most peculiar and charming events take place in the very streets and square of the historical city center, thus transforming the entire city into one big stage.

Bassano and the other stage cities have found a marvelous way to take you on the most spectacular of journeys all throughout the summer in the land of Veneto, through a program of cultural events which supports innovative and artistic ideas while at the same time respecting tradition, and created on purpose for their charming historical, artistic and natural sets. *(Operaestate Festival press office).*

155-158. An international dance ensemble. The most prestigious dance companies come to Bassano from all over the world: an extraordinary exhibition of innovative contemporary dance, including ballet and the most riveting folk dancing. The opera season is produced by the Festival organization and is known for its high quality and detailed productions: elegant sets, musical scores and direction, and a variety of young and talented singers. The Festival also draws great attention to productions of contemporary theatre, providing a stage upcoming companies featuring readings of the classics, the history of the territory and forays in the culinary tradition.

25

A Net of Tourist Suggestions

Asolo, Bassano del Grappa, Castelfranco Veneto, Cittadella, Marostica, and Possagno: six cities united by a large range of itineraries and fantastic offers.

In the heart of Veneto, along the uneven routes that lead to where the plane meets the foothill, there lies the territory of the Hexagon. This region in the middle of the provinces of Padova, Vicenza and Treviso, known all over the world (think of Venice, the Dolomites, the beaches, the thermal spas, the lakes, the historical towns) reveals to all who wish to look deep into its soul its hidden treasures. Here you find six wonderful towns: Asolo, Bassano del Grappa, Castelfranco Veneto, Cittadella, Marostica, and Possagno, all steeped in great historical and cultural heritage, surrounded by the most breathtaking and enchanting landscapes. They all offer excellent reasons to be chosen as a holiday destination year round: the works of great artists (the paintings by Jacopo dal Ponte and Giorgione are exceptionally beautiful, the sculptures by Antonio Canova, and the architectural plans by Palladio) in the numerous museums (more than ten); the locations where episodes of the great world wars took place, the Road of Ceramics, the artistic craftwork, wine and food, and cultural events. The extensive range of proposals and itineraries can be interchanged and connected to make your visit both memorable and exciting. Rich in water, this land offers a magical landscape that makes all that you do pleasurable: strolling through the historical centers or the colorful nature, entering craftsmen's workshops, tasting the traditional dishes, or just attending a show will leave anyone that visit here with the most unforgettable memories. *(Operaestate Festival press office).*

▲ *159-160. Above a nocturnal view of the Castle of Ezzelino. Below, the Ponte Vecchio and the historical center of Bassano on the left bank of the river Brenta.*

161-165. Clockwise, a view of Asolo and its stronghold, an aerial view of Cittadella, the Tempio Canoviano in Possagno, the surrounding walls and the main castle of Marostica, the statue of Giorgione in the historical center of Castelfranco by the river Muson.

Essential Bibliography

Brentari O., *Storia di Bassano e del suo territorio*, Bassano 1884; Magagnato L., Passamani B. (a cura di), *Il Museo Civico di Bassano del Grappa. Dipinti dal XIV al XX secolo*, Neri Pozza, Vicenza 1978; Comitato per la Storia di Bassano (a cura di), *Storia di Bassano*, Tipografia San Giuseppe, Vicenza 1980; Alberton Vinco da Sesso L., Petoello G., *Guida di Bassano del Grappa*, Edizioni Scrimin, Bassano del Grappa 1981; Club Alpino Italiano - Sezione di Bassano del Grappa (a cura di), *Il Grappa. Un patrimonio ambientale*, Tipografia Minchio, Bassano del Grappa 1985; Fasoli G. (a cura di), *Atlante storico delle città italiane. Veneto I. Bassano del Grappa*, Grafo, Bologna 1988; Infelise M., Marini P., *Remondini. Un editore del Settecento*, catalogo della mostra, Electa, Milano 1989; Comitato per la Storia di Bassano (a cura di), *Il Duomo di Santa Maria in Colle di Bassano del Grappa*, Tipografia Rumor, Vicenza 1991; Brown B.L., Marini P. (a cura di), *Jacopo Bassano c. 1510-1592*, catalogo della mostra, Nuova Alpha Editoriale, Bologna 1992; Puppi L. (a cura di), *Il ponte di Bassano*, Vicenza 1993; Avagnina M. E., *Il sorriso dell'Imperatore*, in *Federico. Mito e Memoria*, a cura di Emanuela Angiuli, Biblos, Cittadella 1994; Barbieri G., Olivato L. (a cura di), *Vicenza. I musei del territorio*, Biblos, Cittadella 1995; Alberton Vinco da Sesso L. (a cura di), *Interni bassanesi*, Ghedina e Tassotti, Bassano del Grappa 1996; Del Sal R., Guderzo M. (a cura di), *Mille anni di storia. Bassano 998-1998*, Biblos, Cittadella 1999; Puppi L., *Palladio. L'opera completa*, a cura di Donata Battilotti, Electa, Milano 1999; Signori F., *San Bassiano patrono di Bassano ieri e oggi*, Bertoncello Arti Grafiche, Cittadella 1999; Guderzo M. (a cura di), *Pittura dell'Ottocento e del Novecento*, Terra Ferma, Vicenza 2000; *Bassano nella memoria*, Libreria Palazzo Roberti, Bassano del Grappa 2001; Guderzo M., Rearick W.R., *Jacopo dal Ponte al Museo di Bassano*, Terra Ferma, Vicenza 2001; *Bassano del Grappa. La Torre Civica restaurata,* Intesa BCI - Terra Ferma, Vicenza 2002; *Risalendo la città. Guida all'esposizione permanente nella Torre Civica,* a cura di Renata del Sal e Gaimberto Petoello, Comune di Bassano del Grappa, Cremona, 2003.

Useful Contacts

V.I.P.
Vicenza Information & Promotion
via E. Fermi, 134 - Vicenza
tel. +39 0444 964380 fax +39 0444 994779
e-mail info@vicenzae.org
www.vicenzae.org

Bassano del Grappa Town Hall
Tourist Department Via Vendramini, 35
tel. +39 0424 217810 fax +39 0424 217818
e-mail comune@comune.bassano.vi.it
www.comune.bassano.vi.it

I.A.T. - Tourist Information Office
Province of Vicenza
largo Corona d'Italia, 35
tel. +39 0424 524351 fax +39 0424 525301
e-mail info@vicenzae.org
www.vicenzae.org

Promo Bassano Più
largo Parolini, 52/m
tel. +39 0424 228651 fax +39 0424 525355

Operafestival Office
via Vendramini, 35
tel. +39 0424 217815 fax +39 0424 217813
e-mail operafestival@comune.bassano.vi.it

Pro Bassano
largo Corona d'Italia, 35
tel. fax +39 0424 227580

Museum Archive Library
piazza Garibaldi
tel. +39 0424 519450 fax +39 0424 523914
museobas@x-land.it

Palazzo Sturm
Exhibition of Arts and Crafts of Bassano del Grappa (ceramics, prints)
via Schiavonetti
tel. +39 0424 524933

Other Museums and Halls

Palazzo Bonaguro
via Angarano
tel. +39 0424 502923

Palazzo Agostinelli
via Barbieri
tel. +39 0424 522211

Chiesetta dell'Angelo
via Roma, 80
tel. +39 0424 227303

Museum of the First World War
via Ca' Erizzo, 7
Open from June to September - free entrance
tel. +39 0424 524351

Parking areas

Cadorna
piazzale Cadorna: underground attended parking area, with access to the city center
tel. +39 0424 220673

Gerosa
viale de Gasperi, attended, with free bus service to the city center - free parking
tel. +39 0424 30850

Printed in Italy
by Grafiche Antiga (Cornuda - Italy)
December 2003